Simply Dickens

Simply Dickens

PAUL SCHLICKE

SIMPLY CHARLY
NEW YORK

For Judith and Franny

Contents

Praise for *Simply Dickens*

"This hugely readable book by a distinguished Dickens scholar provides, in less than 100 pages, a remarkably comprehensive, authoritative and vividly written account of Dickens's astonishing life and career. Dr. Schlicke's primary focus is of course on Dickens as a supremely great novelist, and on the roots of his writing in his own personal experiences, but he gives detailed attention also to other aspects of Dickens' life and career such as his travels, editorial work, passion for the theatre, public readings and social activism."
–Michael Slater, Emeritus Professor of Victorian Literature at Birkbeck, past President of the International Dickens Fellowship, and former editor of its journal, *The Dickensian*

"*Simply Dickens* offers a concise account of the multiple lives of Charles Dickens, the author of more memorable characters with distinctive voices than any writer save Shakespeare. Meet the journalist, the philanthropist and social critic, the public speaker, the performer of readings from his own works, the actor and director of plays—they are all here jostling to keep company with the childhood and personal life of the man whose novels have secured his reputation and won readers throughout the world. Paul Schlicke presents this eminently accessible portrait in a series of brief chapters, expertly blending the contours of Dickens's multivalent activities with commentary on his development as a novelist, an author who grows quickly beyond the literary traditions he inherited to develop the unique and powerful prose that defines his major works."
–David Paroissien, Editor of *Dickens Quarterly*

"Paul Schlicke presents us with *Simply Dickens* in all his fascinating complexity. He succeeds in providing readers with a clear outline of the events in Dickens's life, with a shrewd and well-judged critical assessment of his works, including some of the less well-known and less popular, novels and stories. His survey embraces Dickens's journalism, his passion for theatre and performance, his relationship with the age in which he lived and about which he delivered, at times, some severe judgements. The development of Dickens's art is traced through to the works of his maturity, pointing to the way in which his themes and attitudes crystallised and had a clear impact on the honing of his craft as the greatest novelist of the nineteenth century. Alongside this, there emerges a figure who, as Paul Schlicke points out towards the end of this very valuable short study, had an enormous 'appetite' for life and living."

–Dr. Tony Williams, President of The Dickens Fellowship and Associate Editor of *The Dickensian*

"This is one of the best short introductions to Dickens's life and work that I know. Paul Schlicke integrates the life of this extraordinary man with his fiction, journalism and public readings in a very engaging and lively narrative. I wouldn't hesitate to recommend this to the widest range of readers."

–Malcolm Andrews, Emeritus Professor Victorian & Visual Arts, University of Kent, Editor of *The Dickensian*

Other *Great Lives*

Series Editor's Foreword

S imply Charly's "Great Lives" series offers brief but authoritative introductions to the world's most influential people—scientists, artists, writers, economists, and other historical figures whose contributions have had a meaningful and enduring impact on our society.

Each book provides an illuminating look at the works, ideas, personal lives, and the legacies these individuals left behind, also shedding light on the thought processes, specific events, and experiences that led these remarkable people to their groundbreaking discoveries or other achievements. Additionally, every volume explores various challenges they had to face and overcome to make history in their respective fields, as well as the little-known character traits, quirks, strengths, and frailties, myths and controversies that sometimes surrounded these personalities.

Our authors are prominent scholars and other top experts who have dedicated their careers to exploring each facet of their subjects' work and personal lives.

Unlike many other works that are merely descriptions of the major milestones in a person's life, the "Great Lives" series goes above and beyond the standard format and content. It brings substance, depth, and clarity to the sometimes-complex lives and works of history's most powerful and influential people.

We hope that by exploring this series, readers will not only gain new knowledge and understanding of what drove these geniuses, but also find inspiration for their own lives. Isn't this what a great book is supposed to do?

Charles Carlini, Simply Charly
New York City

Preface

In her 1886 memoir titled *My Father as I Recall Him*, Charles Dickens's daughter Mamie described how, being allowed as a convalescent child to remain in his study while he wrote, she observed his activity:

> On one of those mornings, I was lying on the sofa endeavouring to keep perfectly quiet, while my father wrote busily and rapidly at his desk, when he suddenly jumped up from his chair and rushed to a mirror which hung near, and in which I could see the reflections of some extraordinary facial contortions which he was making. He returned rapidly to his desk, wrote furiously for a few moments, and then went again to the mirror. The facial pantomime was resumed, and then turning forward, but evidently not seeing me, he began talking rapidly in a low voice. Ceasing this soon, however, he returned to his desk, where he remained silently writing until lunchtime. It was a most curious experience for me, and one of which I did not until later years, fully appreciate the purport. Then I knew that with his natural intensity he had thrown himself completely into the character that he was creating, and that for the time being he had not only lost sight of his surroundings, but had actually become in action, and in imagination, the creature of his pen.

This description confirms what readers have always recognized in the characters Dickens created, that is, their life-like nature and the extent to which they reflect something intrinsic to Dickens himself. In a speech to the Royal General Theatrical Fund on March 29, 1858, while proposing a toast to his fellow novelist William Makepeace Thackeray, Dickens spoke of the essentially theatrical nature of fiction: "Every writer of fiction," he said, "though he may not adopt the dramatic form, writes in effect for the stage." Whatever interpretation one might wish to make of this statement as a feature in fiction generally, there can be no question of its applicability to Dickens's own writing. His characters are theatrical in the sense that they invariably declaim and act as if performing on a stage, their essence belonging to the author who created them. This gives them a vital, histrionic presence, as vivid as any personages in any novel ever written. If this means that his characters seem to lack the inwardness we find in the works of other great writers, they more than make up for any limitations in that regard by their vital presence, as Dickens the actor impersonates them on the page.

Moreover—and this is the important point about his life as well as his art—Dickens was, to an unusual degree, a multi-faceted man, who took on a wide variety of roles in his everyday activities. He threw himself wholeheartedly into everything he did. Wrenched from school at an early age on account of his father's financial troubles, he was sent to work in a boot-blacking warehouse, a fate which he thought at the time would dash any aspirations he had for a better future and consign him to manual labor for the rest of his life—unless, he feared, he would end up as a little vagabond. After two stints as a clerk in law offices, Dickens became a newspaper reporter and quickly established himself as an expert parliamentary journalist. He continued to write for newspapers and journals for the rest of his life and to act as editor for a number of periodicals. He went to the theater constantly in those early days, secured an appointment for an audition at Covent Garden Theatre Royal, and might have made a career as an actor but for the steady success he had achieved by then as a journalist. However, Dickens retained a vital interest in the theater, as playgoer, reviewer, playwright, actor, producer, manager, and eventually public reader of his own works. His first forays into fiction, published as magazine and newspaper sketches, became phenomenally popular, and the longer fictions which followed quickly established him as the foremost novelist of the age—indeed, of all time. His writings about Christmas—"A Christmas Dinner" in *Sketches by Boz*, the Dingley Dell episode in

Pickwick, and "A Christmas Carol"–among them–associated Dickens's name with that holiday; it was even said that when he died, one little girl asked if that meant Father Christmas would die too.

After a childhood infatuation with a little neighborhood girl in Chatham, as a young man Dickens fell in love, was jilted, and married on the rebound. Years later, in his mid-40s and at the height of his fame, he fell madly in love once more. However, his marriage, which had produced 10 children, eventually collapsed and, permanently estranged from his wife, he led a secret life with a woman young enough to be his daughter. He traveled for extended periods to Italy, Switzerland, France, and North America, writing travel books arising from his experiences. Dickens also campaigned actively for a variety of social causes and, for a decade, without easing up on any other activities, he worked tirelessly as factotum for a wealthy heiress, overseeing the daily running of a refuge for homeless women. In the midst of all this intense and varied activity, he wrote 14 novels of unparalleled genius and was midway through the 15th when, at the early age of 58, he died of a massive stroke.

Dickens's favorite performer was an actor named Charles Mathews, famous for impersonating a series of characters in one-man shows known as "monopolylogues." Dickens's own public readings were notable for the number of roles he undertook in each reading as if he actually embodied all the characters whose lines he recited. Every one of the hundreds of fictive personages who populate his works partakes to a greater or lesser extent in the inner life of their author. In his art and in his life, it was indeed as if Dickens led multiple lives; certainly, he expended more energy in greater diversity than many other men.

In the pages that follow, we will survey the multivalent activities of this remarkable man.

Paul Schlicke
Aberdeen, Scotland

Acknowledgements

A special thanks to William F. Long, for many fruitful discussions about Dickens over many years, and for his reading of the manuscript. I would also like to thank Malcolm Andrews, Michael Slater, David Paroissien, and Tony Williams, each of whom read the manuscript and made helpful suggestions. Any errors which remain are, of course, solely my responsibility.

Cast of Characters

The Schoolboy – Mr. Charles Dickens!

The Lover as child – Mr. Charles Dickens!

The Labouring Hind – Mr. Charles Dickens!

The Law Clerk – Mr. Charles Dickens!

The Reporter – Mr. Charles Dickens!

The Dandy Lover – Mr. Charles Dickens!

Boz – Mr. Charles Dickens!

The Playwright – Mr. Charles Dickens!

The Editor – Mr. Charles Dickens!

The Novelist – Mr. Charles Dickens!

Father Christmas – Mr. Charles Dickens!

The International Traveller – Mr. Charles Dickens!

The Autobiographer – Mr. Charles Dickens!

The Social Activist – Mr. Charles Dickens!

The Mature Lover – Mr. Charles Dickens!

Roscius – Mr. Charles Dickens!

The Colossus – Mr. Charles Dickens!

1. "Almost a little vagabond"

Some of Dickens's most poignant journalistic writing evoked reminiscences of himself as a child. He was also the first great novelist who wrote extensively about childhood—creating characters like Oliver Twist, Little Nell, Tiny Tim, Paul Dombey, David Copperfield, and Philip Pirrip (known as Pip). We don't know to what extent these writings drew upon actual events in his life, but one thing is certain: the emotional experiences described in his books stemmed from his own memories. One of the most touching pieces is the 1853 sketch "Gone Astray," which depicted Dickens as a youngster separated from his adult companion:

> When I was a very small boy indeed, both in years and stature, I got lost one day in the City of London. I was taken out by Somebody (shade of Somebody forgive me for remembering no more of thy identity!), as an immense treat, to be shown the outside of St. Giles's church.

The sketch proceeds to recount solitary adventures on that fateful day, with an intensity of feeling, which stamps them with the authenticity of events as they really happened. The boy befriends a dog, which ungraciously snatches his saveloy (sausage); he observes the giant statues of Gog and Magog at the Guildhall, and he wanders into a theater, where he becomes alarmed at the prospect of winning a donkey, which is being raffled off. The experiences epitomize key elements of Dickens's conception of childhood: solitary, observant, sensitive, hopeful, full of wonder—as well as terror—at the fearsome immensity and otherness of the world beyond his own little self. It is a marvelously compelling image, one of the triumphs of Dickens's artistry, but it is not only an image: it is also a narrative stance, which allowed him to see with vivid freshness, pathos, and humor.

What personal, life-altering experiences had made it possible for young Dickens to develop such profound insight into the workings of a child's mind?

Charles John Huffam Dickens was born on February 7, 1812, at 13 Mile End Terrace, Portsea (now 396 Commercial Road, Portsmouth, home of the Dickens Birthplace Museum), a suburb of a great naval port then servicing wars in two hemispheres, against Napoleon on the continent and against the United States in America. His mother, Elizabeth Barrow Dickens, was said to have been dancing at a ball the night before her first son and second child was born, and his father, John Dickens, held a responsible position in the naval pay office. The job took the family first to London and then to the dockyards at Chatham, at the junction of the Medway with the Thames.

It was in Chatham that young Dickens experienced the happiest days of his childhood, playing imaginative games with neighborhood friends in the field across the street from the family home in Ordnance Terrace, and falling desperately in love with a little girl named Lucy Stroughill. "Dullborough Town" [1860] is his fictionalized evocation of those joyful days:

> Here, in the haymaking time, had I been delivered from the dungeons of Seringapatam, an immense pile (of haycock), by my countrymen, the victorious British (boy next door and his two cousins), and had been recognised with ecstasy by my affianced one (Miss Green), who had come all the way from England (second house in the terrace), to ransom me, and marry me.

In Chatham, Dickens had been schooled by his mother, and later under the tutelage of a schoolmaster, the Rev. William Giles, whom he remembered fondly in later years. During this time, he began (like David Copperfield in his childhood) to read voraciously ("as if for life"), novels and essays above all, and to listen with rapt attention to the terrifying stories, such as Captain Murderer, told by his nursemaid Mary Weller. It was in those days too, that he first saw Gad's Hill Place, on walks with his father, who told him that if he worked hard enough, he might one day live in that big house—as he did, many years later.

The childhood idyll ended abruptly when Dickens's father was transferred back to London, where financial difficulties led to several moves of house to escape creditors. His beloved older sister Fanny was funded to continue her studies at the Royal Academy of Music, but there was not enough money to allow young Dickens to continue his education, and around the time of his 12th birthday an event occurred, which Dickens (and most of his biographers) considered to be the formative trauma of his life. He was sent to work pasting labels on bottles of bootblacking while sitting in a window, exposed to the gaze of passers-by. Soon after he started the work, his father was arrested for debt, and the rest of the family moved to the Marshalsea Debtors' Prison in Borough High Street while young Dickens lived in lodgings in nearby Lant Street. The alienation he felt was signaled by the fact that he adopted the name of a boy who befriended him at the blacking factory—Bob Fagin—for the nightmarish villain of *Oliver Twist*.

The actual employment lasted about a year, but to the boy himself, it seemed the end of the world.

> It is wonderful to me [he wrote later] how I could have been so easily cast away at such an age. . . No words can express the secret agony of my soul . . . my early hopes of growing up to be a learned and distinguished man, crushed in my breast. The deep remembrance of the sense I had of being utterly neglected and hopeless . . . My whole nature . . . penetrated with the grief and humiliation . . . I know that, but for the mercy of God, I might easily have been, for any care that was taken of me, a little robber or a little vagabond.

After a few months, his father was released from prison, quarreled with the factory manager, and withdrew young Dickens from his employment. His mother tried to patch up the dispute, and, as Dickens wrote:

> I never afterwards forgot, I shall never forget, I never can forget that my mother was warm for my being sent back.

The trauma was long-lasting. Deeply ashamed, Dickens kept the experience secret; it did not become public knowledge until his intimate friend and biographer John Forster made the revelation after Dickens's death. Because of this early trauma, Dickens had a morbid sensitivity and fear of failure, coupled with an iron determination to succeed at whatever he did and avoid any possibility of financial difficulty. It gave him a sense of self-sufficiency, a readiness to depend on no one but himself for anything he undertook. Above all, it gave him a perception of childhood as an idyllic state irrevocably lost; it also fostered in him the essential need to never outgrow the child's sense of wonder.

Afterward, Dickens resumed schooling briefly, at Wellington House Academy, under a schoolmaster whom he later described as "by far the most ignorant man I have ever had the pleasure to know. "Our school," he recalled, "was remarkable for white mice:"

> The boys trained the mice much better than the masters taught the boys. We recall one white mouse, who lived in the cover of a Latin dictionary, who ran up ladders, drew Roman chariots, shouldered muskets, turned wheels, and even made a very creditable appearance on the stage as the dog of Montargis. He might have achieved greater things, but for having the misfortune to mistake his way in a triumphal procession to the Capitol, when he fell into a deep inkstand, and was dyed black and drowned.

Dickens was always the leader in such activities. While still very young, he and his sister Fanny would use a table for a stage in the Mitre Tavern in Rochester to sing duets. "At the mature age of eight or ten," he recalled in his Preface to the 1850 edition of *Sketches by Boz*, he composed his first attempts at authorship, "certain tragedies achieved and represented with great applause to overflowing nurseries," one of which was *Misnar, the Sultan of India*, based on his beloved *Arabian Nights*. His lifelong fascination with the theater began early, leading to discovery of "many wondrous secrets of nature . . . not the least terrific were, that the witches in Macbeth bore an awful resemblance to the Thanes and other proper inhabitants of Scotland, and that the good King Duncan couldn't rest in his grave, but was constantly coming out of it, and calling himself somebody else." His toy theater production of *The Miller and His Men* resulted in the police being called when the explosion at the finale was too realistic.

After school, Dickens had found employment as an office boy, first with the law firm of Ellis and Blackmore of Gray's Inn, and subsequently with the solicitor Charles Molloy of Symonds Inn. On his first day, resplendent in a new blue coat and a military-looking cap, Dickens responded to the taunts of a bully and turned up in the office with a black eye. He amused himself by dropping cherry stones out of the window on the hats of passers-by, and during those years, he started going to the theater frequently, sometimes paying to take on roles on private stages, as later described in one of the *Sketches by Boz*.

At this time, another devastating event occurred in Dickens's life. Only recently discovered and previously thought to relate to a far earlier time, its significance can hardly be overstated. Dickens's youngest sister Harriet, not quite nine years old, died on August 19, 1827, long after the family's move from Chatham and years after the days at the blacking warehouse. Biographers have up to now pointed to the sudden death a decade later of his 17-year-old sister-in-law Mary Hogarth, as the event which precipitated Dickens's preoccupation with childhood death, but it seems probable that the passing of Harriet must have had prior impact on her 15-year old brother. His 1850 sketch "A Child's Dream of a Star" recounting the death of a sister "very young, oh very very young" fits Harriet far better than either Mary or his older sister Fanny, who died in 1848 at 38. Central to his art, Dickens's conception of childhood as precious was emphatically reinforced by his experience that it was also precarious.

2. Here Comes Boz!

In his Preface to the 1847 edition of *The Pickwick Papers*, Dickens recalled his feelings on the publication of the first of his sketches in December 1833, when he was only 21 years old:

> . . . my first effusion, dropped stealthily one evening at twilight, with fear and trembling, into a dark letter-box, in a dark office, up a dark court in Fleet Street appeared in all the glory of print; on which occasion, by the bye,–how well I recollect it!–I walked down to Westminster Hall, and turned into it for half-an-hour, because my eyes were so dimmed with joy and pride, that they could not bear the street, and were not fit to be seen there.

The joy recorded in this retrospective account of the launch of his career as a writer was no doubt genuine, but it obscures the fact that there was nothing inevitable about the path Dickens was to take. He seriously considered other options, both then and later.

A legal career was one possibility. Having been employed as a clerk in law offices after he left school, he subsequently lived for two years in Furnival's Inn, which had formerly been one of the lesser Inns of Court, which served as the institutional home of the legal profession. By the time Dickens moved in, the buildings had been converted into private residences, but on applying for residence there in 1834, he declared that he intended to study law. Given the series of less than flattering portraits he later drew of lawyers–Dodson and Fogg in *Pickwick*, Mr. Spenlow in *Copperfield*, Vholes and Tulkinghorn in *Bleak House*–this ambition seems surprising, to say the least. But in December 1839, he paid the fee of £33 8s and was admitted as a student of Middle Temple Inn of Court. He reaffirmed his intention to pursue the law career in 1846, expressing desire to become a police magistrate, but gave up on this plan in 1855. Although Dickens was outspoken in his conviction that writing was a profession requiring commitment—which he thought was lacking in his rival William Makepeace Thackeray—it is astonishing to think that he could nevertheless contemplate a career change at the age of 43.

The stage was a second distinct possibility. He told Forster that he attended theaters as a young man "almost every night for a long time," particularly to see the solo performances of Charles Mathews. Dickens studied and practiced, then wrote to the stage manager at the Theatre at Covent Garden and was granted an audition. However, falling ill on the day, he missed the appointment and, being fully occupied with newspaper reporting soon thereafter, did not renew the application. Still in his early 20s, he wrote several plays, hoping to make his name as a dramatist; he made close, life-long friendships with actors and playwrights, above all with the pre-eminent tragedian William Charles Macready, and even staged a number of amateur theatrical performances with considerable success. Eventually, as we shall see, he devoted the final 12 years of his life to his own highly individualized amalgam of writing and acting, performing public readings from his works to huge acclaim. Macready, who had a low opinion of amateur acting, confided to his diary that Dickens could have been a fine actor.

But the path on which he first embarked, and which he followed for the rest of his life, even when other activities intervened, was journalism. During his incarceration in the Marshalsea, Dickens's father had retired from the Admiralty and on release from prison took a job as a newspaper correspondent, a career that he followed successfully for the rest of his life. Encouraged to follow in his father's footsteps, young Dickens, still in his teens, taught himself shorthand and initially worked freelance, supplying penny-a-line copy to the paper for which his father worked, the *British Press*. After leaving the law offices, he found employment with a weekly paper owned by his maternal uncle John Henry Barrow, *The Mirror of Parliament*, at the time a superior rival to *Hansard* as a record of parliamentary debates. Dickens soon made a name for himself with the speed and accuracy of his reporting, and for a brief spell worked simultaneously on an evening paper, the *True Sun*. "There never was such a short-hand-writer," claimed Thomas Beard, a fellow journalist who became a life-long friend. Sitting in the cramped gallery, Dickens heard and transcribed debates concerning some of the monumental legislative events of the century: the Reform Bill, Catholic emancipation, and the abolition of slavery in the colonies.

In 1834, Dickens graduated to a more prestigious job with the Whig *Morning Chronicle*, rival to the Tory *Times*. His editor, John Black, recognized his potential; "my first hearty out-and-out appreciator," Dickens later recalled. He was responsible for routine reporting, theater reviews, and coverage of electoral hustings—meetings at which candidates for a political office addressed potential voters. For all his later fame as a novelist, he never abandoned his activities as a journalist, contributing articles and letters, editing monthly and weekly periodicals, and even briefly editing a daily newspaper. Moreover, all of his novels were first published serially before being collected in volume form. Dickens's vocation as a journalist lasted his entire lifetime and was integral to his achievements as a creative writer.

His early work as a parliamentary correspondent meant that his reporting was intermittent, needed only when the House was in session. That left him seeking other employment during times of recess, with momentous results. His first imaginative piece to be published (without payment and without a byline) was "A Dinner at Poplar Walk" (later substantially revised as "Mr. Minns and His Cousin"), which appeared in December 1833 in the ardently Reform-orientated *Monthly Magazine*. Over the next three years, he wrote some 60 sketches (eight of which were combined in pairs, adding up to the total of 56), which attracted widespread interest in the press, leading to literally hundreds of notices. Paragraphs or larger segments from the sketches were frequently excerpted, and nearly every one of them was reprinted in its entirety, sometimes several times over, in different papers. When the first series of 37 sketches, accompanied by etchings by the foremost book illustrator of the day, George Cruikshank, was published in two volumes by John

Macrone in February 1836, the work was promptly pirated in Philadelphia and Paris, and not long after in Calcutta, Leipzig, and Boston. Dickens was not merely the talk of the town, but also the talk of the English-speaking world. It is not widely recognized that this reception of his earliest published work was stupendous: reviewers promptly compared him favorably with Sir Walter Scott, Henry Fielding, and Miguel de Cervantes; they praised his sharpness of observation, the distinctive inventiveness of his style, exuberance, humor, pathos, range, and variety of tone. Because the reception of *Pickwick* less than a year later eclipsed the reputation of the sketches, and because Dickens himself quickly became dissatisfied with them—revising extensively on several occasions and apologizing for their imperfections in prefaces—they are generally seen only as apprentice work. But as Forster wisely observed, "the first sprightly runnings of his genius are undoubtedly here," and they immediately established his reputation as a literary giant.

The narrative sketches, gathered together as "Tales" in 1839, followed in all subsequent editions, and dealt with comic misadventure, often reflecting the precarious respectability of Dickens's own youthful experience, the perils of social aspiration, and the vicissitudes of daily life. "Doctors' Commons" and "Criminal Courts" drew on his legal as well as journalistic experience. The "Our Parish" sketches provided a microcosm of England in the 1830s, and the Gothic horrors of "The Black Veil" and "The Drunkard's Death" extended the tonal range. But the non-narrative "Scenes" and "Characters" were uniquely distinguished. The alert eye of Boz—the pseudonym, pronounced "baws," was a pet name in the family—satirically probed incongruity and affectation, even as his genial persona invited deep sympathy for people he surveyed. The subtitle, "Illustrative of Every-day Life and Every-day People," not only defined Dickens's subject matter, but also pointed to a vigorously political stance in the Reform era, opposing elitist condescension of wealth and status, and taking the activities and aspirations of the unenfranchised majority of ordinary men and women seriously. At once reportage and invention, realism and theatricality, satire and celebration, *Sketches by Boz* is a minor masterpiece.

Two events immediately followed the publication of the first volumes of Dickens's sketches. He was approached the very next day by the publishers Chapman and Hall, who invited him to contribute to a projected serial. With regular income secured, Dickens got married. For two years he had been smitten with Maria Beadnell, the daughter of a prosperous banker. She toyed with his affections, and her father was unimpressed with her suitor's prospects. After the frustration of fruitless courtship, Dickens gave up and on the rebound married Catherine Hogarth, whose father had recruited him in 1835 to write a series of sketches for the newly launched *Evening Chronicle*. He was never as fervent in courting Catherine as he had been with Maria—his letters to Catherine reveal that, above all, he was striving to make a name for himself—and he later claimed that he and Catherine had never been suited for one another. However, all the evidence suggests that Dickens was an affectionate husband, and that the marriage had been happy for many years. Catherine shared Dickens's sense of fun; her poise and charm impressed all observers. She acted in one of his amateur theatrical productions and published a collection of menus, indicative of Dickens's culinary tastes (and his partiality for toasted cheese). Although Catherine suffered from illness and depression after the birth of each of their 10 children, she managed the household, entertained his guests, and bravely accompanied Dickens on many of his travels.

In April 1837, Dickens, Catherine, and their first-born infant, Charley, moved to their first house, a three-story Georgian mansion at 48 Doughty Street (now the Charles Dickens Museum). Catherine's younger sister Mary was often with them, sharing their happiness, until suddenly one night, after an outing to the theater, 17-year-old Mary fell ill and died the next morning in Dickens's arms. Catherine suffered a miscarriage from the shock, and Dickens missed publishers' deadlines. Prompted by his extravagant expressions of grief, critics and biographers have speculated darkly ever since about an affair between Dickens and his sister-in-law, but there is absolutely nothing to suggest a liaison of this kind. But after Mary's death, Dickens the novelist projected back onto her all the possible feelings a man might have for an attractive young woman. Moreover, as previously suggested, Dickens's experience of the passing of his sister Harriet several years earlier was a prior inspiration for many of his depictions of childhood death.

The Pickwick Papers, projected as a series of comic engravings of cockney sporting life, was initially conceived by the established graphic illustrator Robert Seymour. Dickens was hired to supply letterpress—hackwork, which his friends advised against. Seymour's idea was of a "Nimrod Club" in which members would suffer comic misadventures while fishing and shooting, but Dickens objected that the concept was hardly novel and, in any case, he was "no great sportsman." He sought a "freer range of scenes and people," as he had done in his sketches, and promptly took control of the project. "I thought of Mr. Pickwick and wrote the first number," Dickens observed in the 1847 Preface as if the conception had emerged spontaneously from his imagination. In fact, the story is steeped in tradition, as Dickens drew on his reading of 18th-century novels, plays, and periodicals. Joseph Addison and Richard Steele's "Spectator Club," a group of male friends convivially exchanging stories, adventures, and reminiscences, appealed strongly to him, not only for this project, but also in his conception for Master Humphrey's Clock and in his later membership in several gentlemen's clubs, starting with the Cerebus Club—exclusive to Dickens, Forster and Harrison Ainsworth—and later in the Garrick Club, as well as the Athenaeum.

The project was no sooner underway than Seymour committed suicide, after finishing only a handful of etchings. Sales were negligible, and Robert Buss, hired to replace the artist, proved unsatisfactory—Thackeray had applied for the job but was turned down. The sensible thing for the publishers in these circumstances would have been to abandon the venture as a failure, but they persevered. Hablot Browne was hired as illustrator, Dickens introduced Sam Weller in the fourth installment, and the work became the publishing sensation of the 19th century. Before it completed its serial run of 20 numbers, there were, at least, five stage adaptations in London alone; Pickwick hats, Sam Weller corduroys, china figurines, songbooks, and sub-literary imitations became popular. And for over half a century, a standard repertoire piece in the circus was a quick-change routine on horseback, in which the artist portrayed a sequence of characters from the story: Tony Weller, Mr. Pickwick, the Fat Boy, and Sam Weller.

"Dickens went into the Pickwick Club to scoff, and Dickens remained to pray." So judged G. K. Chesterton, one of the most perceptive of all Dickens's critics. It is certainly true that Mr. Pickwick was introduced as the butt of jokes, and before the story's end, the mutually supportive relationship between Sam and his master had transformed the tone to one of warm affection. The story charts the adventures of Mr. Pickwick and his friends as they traveled about England, and it developed the characters of Mr. Pickwick's insouciant manservant Sam and Sam's corpulent father Tony, with an aversion to "widders." Nine stories in which characters relate to one another intermittently, interrupt the narrative, several radically darkening the overall tone. Critics have debated about the "education" of Mr. Pickwick, and Dickens himself allowed that he became "better acquainted" with the character as the story proceeded; be that as it may, in the combination of Mr. Pickwick's innocent benevolence and Sam's worldly wisdom, Dickens achieved something utterly magical and infinitely engaging. And although he later judged that his public wouldn't take another Pickwick from him, around half of the vast amount of material written about Dickens for the rest of the 19th century was in celebration of The Pickwick Papers.

In February 1837, barely halfway through the serial run of Pickwick, Oliver Twist began appearing in a new monthly periodical, Bentley's Miscellany, which Dickens was editing. Dickens was committing himself to the composition of two extended serialized narratives simultaneously. In all probability, he was considering writing this novel as early as 1833, and certainly, its opening scenes portraying activities in a rural parish bear basic congruence with "Our Parish" in *Sketches by Boz.* With its trenchant satire of the Poor Law and dark scenes of London's criminal underworld, *Oliver Twist* contrasts markedly with the sunny adventures of Mr. Pickwick and his companions.

In *Oliver Twist*, Dickens confronted a burning issue of the day, the system of parish relief for those unable to support themselves. In 1834, the New Poor Law was doctrinaire legislation, designed to reduce taxes through a system of "less eligibility." It meant that relief for the impoverished would not exceed the lowest wages of a man in employment—which was, in fact, below the subsistence level. In its focus on the able-bodied, the law evinced scant concern for the needs of orphans, as well as the sick and disabled. To Dickens, such a philosophy was so much cant, and in stark allegory, he cut through its principled rationale by focusing on a single, helpless, unindividuated child, who, devoid of a name of his own—Mr. Bumble, "quite a literary character," invents names alphabetically, with Twist following Swubble—asks humbly for more: not just more gruel, as Dickens makes clear, but more care, more clothing, more dignity, and more love. In its stark simplicity, the image offers a powerful instance of satire. And when, not long after, Oliver runs away and gravitates with inexorable logic to Fagin's den, the message is categorical: a political system based on the logic of the Poor Law leads straight to crime. In a savagely comic rhetoric, Fagin spells out the Utilitarian rationale of the law, when he explains to Noah Claypole that self-interest is the basis of social harmony [chapter 43].

The book is structured in polarities, which Graham Greene described as "Manichean"—that is, the total separation of the principles of good and evil. Dickens spelled out the method in his most overt statement of his literary principles, when he compared "all good, murderous melodrama" to "a side of streaky, well-cured bacon" [chapter 17]. In contrast, the characters of Mr. Brownlow and the Maylies pale into dimness, but the depiction of underworld characters is vivid. Fagin ("such an out and outer that I don't know what to make of him," Dickens confessed to Forster) is the suave devil of folklore, whose last night alive, before he is hanged, is lurid. The Artful Dodger is a comic image of the ultimate alienated outsider; Nancy is the whore with a heart of gold, and in the brutal Sikes, Dickens explores the tortured psyche of a damned soul, pursued relentlessly by the eyes of the woman he has murdered. There are rough edges in the book, to be sure, but also some of Dickens's greatest writing.

The runaway success of *Pickwick* made its publishers, Chapman and Hall, eager for more work by Dickens. On November 18, 1837, the day after *Pickwick* was published in one volume, a contract was signed for a work "of similar character and of the same extent and content in point of quantity"—even though *Oliver Twist* still had a year to run before it appeared in volume form, and six more months beyond that before it completed its serial run. Significantly, the contract did not specify that the new work was to be a novel; at the time they were being written, the generic status of Dickens's extended narratives was problematic for all concerned. This was the case until 1841, when *Barnaby Rudge*, overtly conceived as a historical novel in the manner of Scott, settled the matter.

In January 1838, two months before he began serial publication of *Nicholas Nickleby*, Dickens and his *Pickwick* illustrator, Hablot Browne ("Phiz"), undertook a whirlwind trip to Yorkshire to see for themselves a school there, notorious as a dumping ground for unwanted children. The first adventure in *Nicholas Nickleby* depicts the hero finding employment in the grotesquely horrible Dotheboys Hall, run by the one-eyed ogre of a schoolmaster, Wackford Squeers. In this way, *Nickleby* followed *Twist* by opening with trenchant social satire on a topical issue, and while the Poor Law continued its course until long after Dickens's death, the Yorkshire schools had largely disappeared after their exposure in *Nickleby*. In this work, Dickens followed the well-traveled precedent of 18th-century "life and adventures" fiction, centered on a young hero and organized in loosely-contrasting scenes. In some of the sunniest comedy Dickens ever wrote he described how, after the midwinter travails in the north of England, in the summer Nicholas travels south to Portsmouth, where he joins the itinerant theatrical company of Vincent Crummles. In both episodes, he has romantic encounters, first with the nasty Fanny Squeers and then with the charming actress Miss Snevellicci, but it is not until his return to London to rescue his sister Kate from the machinations of their villainous uncle Ralph, that he finds true love with Madeline Bray. Dickens's heroines are a mixed lot, with most of them among the least interesting of his otherwise superlatively imagined characters, and Madeline Bray is undoubtedly the most pathetically vacuous of them all.

After leaving the Crummleses, Nicholas finds congenial employment with the Cheeryble twins, rescues his sister from an aristocratic would-be seducer, deals manfully with his comically garrulous mother, and foils the machinations of Squeers, Ralph, and various lesser villains before marrying his true love and retiring, along with his sister and her true love, to their late father's rural retreat. The London scenes are filled with a host of comically engaging characters, loosely united by a conventional plot. *Nicholas Nickleby* is a prime example of what Henry James derided as a "large, loose, baggy monster" of a novel, and all the more enjoyable (to those with more expansive taste in fiction) for its sprawling variety.

3. Boz as Editor

I n August 1836, as the first series of *Sketches by Boz* was being reprinted in a second edition, and with *Pickwick* on the brink of its sensational fame, Richard Bentley, the foremost publisher of fiction in Britain, invited Dickens to sign an agreement to write a novel under his imprint. This contract led to further negotiations and a formal commitment by Dickens to write not one but two novels for Bentley, and to take on the job of editing a new humorous periodical, to be launched in the new year. This deal testified to Dickens's early stature, but it was a serious over-commitment, even for an energetic and ambitious young man like Dickens. Something had to give, and it soon did.

Dickens was working full-time as a reporter and author of new weekly sketches for the *Morning Chronicle*. At the same time, he had also agreed to furnish sketches for the *Carlton Chronicle* and to write a children's book for the publisher Thomas Tegg. Already under contract to Macrone to provide enough new sketches for a second series of *Sketches by Boz* and to produce a three-volume novel to be called *Gabriel Varden*, Dickens resigned from the *Morning Chronicle*. The book for Tegg was abandoned as well. He gathered previously overlooked sketches for a single volume (instead of the projected two) for the second series of *Sketches*. When Macrone tried to hold Dickens to his contract for *Gabriel Varden* and started advertising its imminent publication, Dickens became furious. Under duress he sold the copyright of the sketches to Macrone for a paltry sum, just to be released from the contract for *Gabriel Varden*. The publisher died less than a year later, at the tragically young age of 28, and Dickens organized a collection of short fiction by various authors, *The Pic Nic Papers*, to raise money for Macrone's widow.

Chapman and Hall, meantime, showered Dickens with presents, bonuses, and a banquet in his honor, as the commercial value of their prodigy grew enormously. Bentley, in contrast, tried scrupulously to hold to the precise terms of his contracts with Dickens, even deducting payment when episodes of Oliver Twist filled less than a full page. Over the next several months, Dickens wrested no fewer than eight revisions to his original contract with Bentley, including an agreement that Oliver Twist would count both as his monthly contribution to the Miscellany, and as one of the contracted novels—meaning, in effect, that Dickens was paid twice for the same pieces of writing. But if Bentley had reason for exasperation—Dickens's ferocious polemical satire on the Poor Law was a far cry from the genial humor expected from the popular comic writer of Pickwick—Dickens too was getting increasingly frustrated. The reason was not just that contracts did not reflect his rocketing commercial value, but also his lack of editorial control: Bentley routinely inserted text without consulting his editor. Relations became frosty, with Dickens fulminating and calling his employer a "brigand" and "Jew." He completed writing Oliver Twist in November 1838, whereupon it was published in three volumes. Days later, Dickens "burst the Bentleian bonds" by resigning as editor, although the serial continued in the Miscellany until the following April.

Oliver Twist was Dickens's primary contribution to Bentley's Miscellany, but he also wrote several other occasional pieces, including the "Mudfog Papers," satirizing the British Association for the Advancement of Science; "The Pantomime of Life," on the theatricality of everyday life; and "Some Particulars Concerning a Lion," about literary celebrity. The contents of the Miscellany were entirely original, written by numerous contributors, most of whom are wholly forgotten today. Illustrations were done by George Cruikshank, with whom Dickens had collaborated when the Sketches by Boz collection was published in volume form. His friend Ainsworth succeeded him as editor, whose serial contribution, Jack Sheppard, dealing with the adventures of a notorious thief and prison-breaker, ran alongside the final installments of Oliver Twist, leading to both stories being lumped together as "Newgate" novels, criticized for glamorizing crime.

Undeterred by the acrimony between himself and Bentley, Dickens continued to hanker after the challenge of editing a popular periodical. *Pickwick* had been presented under the guise of manuscript documents written by Club members, arranged and presented by Boz as editor; *Memoirs of Grimaldi* (1838) was hackwork undertaken for Bentley, who had acquired the papers of the pantomime clown. In July 1839, as *Nickleby* neared completion, Dickens proposed as his next project with Chapman and Hall a new weekly miscellany, entitled *Master Humphrey's Clock*, to be written by various authors. The central conceit was a cache of sketches, essays, and letters stored in the case of a grandfather clock by a benign old cripple, who was to select and read from the papers to a small group of friends. Concerned that he would burn himself out by writing too much too rapidly, and that his public might tire of his extended narratives, Dickens made certain that the contract he signed gave him full editorial control and dictated that the primary earnings would be his rather than the publishers'.

The conception drew on Dickens's love of 18th-century essayists and the framed tales of *The Arabian Nights*, and marked a return to his earlier success as a sketch writer. In the parlous social circumstances of the time—disillusion with Reform, civil unrest, and the uncertainty about the inexperienced young Queen Victoria (only 18 when she ascended the throne)—a journal of comfortable, old-fashioned storytelling seemed an attractive proposition, but it quickly proved to be a major mistake. The editorial persona of the lugubrious Master Humphrey was unattractive in itself, and as the narrator, he lacked the flexibility enjoyed by Boz. Despite the promise of variety, the opening numbers betrayed a sameness of tone, and the re-introduction of Mr. Pickwick, Sam and Tony Weller fell flat. Initial high sales plummeted in the next numbers, and (not for the last time in his career) Dickens leaped to the rescue. He expanded the sketch featured in the fourth issue depicting the encounter late at night of Master Humphrey with a solitary little girl, whom the old man guided home to a curiosity shop in which she lived among the grotesque objects with her grandfather. The image, grounded in dynamic contrast, took vigorous hold of Dickens's imagination and after the seventh issue, the tale of Little Nell took over as the *Clock's* sole story. Dickens swiftly and unceremoniously jettisoned Master Humphrey as the narrator, and although he attempted to return to the original concept at the story's conclusion by identifying the Single Gentleman (Little Nell's great-uncle) as Master Humphrey himself, the dissimilarity between the two characters was so extreme that the claim utterly lacked credibility. In ensuing issues, *Master Humphrey's Clock* became the vehicle for a second extended narrative, *Barnaby Rudge* (the new title of the long-delayed *Gabriel Varden*), and at the end of that story, the periodical folded.

The two novels in *Master Humphrey's Clock* represented a watershed in Dickens's artistry and an important step in his development as a novelist. Like his earlier extended works of fiction, *The Old Curiosity Shop* followed 18th century precedent in charting the travels of its protagonist through a contrasting variety of scenes. The basically episodic structure dealt with a cast of characters of modest respectability (or no respectability at all), in a predominantly realistic setting, with a strong moral bias and an overt tendency towards representativeness and allegory. The quintessentially Dickensian touch was the focus on a child and the inclusion of low-life entertainers. Little Nell caught the imagination of Dickens's contemporaries and the work firmly consolidated his status as the foremost popular author of his day. He drew directly on a century-old tradition of sentimental literature, evoking the pathos of his heroine's lot and grounding his outlook on feeling rather than intellect. Like Oliver, Nell was a static representative of the sensitive, persecuted child, but unlike Oliver, she was unable to survive in a hostile world. The evocation of her suffering and death incited contemptuous ridicule in later generations ("One must have a heart of stone to read the death of Little Nell without laughing," quipped Oscar Wilde) but Dickens's first readers admired her fortitude and saw her life as exemplary; in Forster's words, it was a kind of "discipline of feeling."

"Everything in our lives, whether of good or evil, affects us most by contrast," Dickens wrote in chapter 53, and his heroine was juxtaposed with the most extraordinary character he ever invented, the demonic dwarf Quilp. An amalgam of fairy tale ogre, Punch and Judy puppet, medieval Vice figure, with a whiff of Byronic alienation and a touch of Shakespeare's Richard III, Quilp had just enough realistic basis to exist as a human character. He gleefully torments everyone he comes in contact with, and his frenetic malice drives him to a gruesome, isolated death simultaneously with Nell's peaceful passing, surrounded by friends.

What marked a new departure for Dickens was neither Nell nor Quilp, but his characterization of Dick Swiveller, the insouciant gent who enters the tale as a cheerful reprobate given to theatrical posturing and quotation from popular song. "I mean to make much of him," Dickens told Forster, and the careless wastrel provides much of the book's happiest comedy. Something more happens when, halfway through the story, Swiveller encounters a starving, nameless waif, whom he names and befriends, and in so doing transforms her into a heroine capable of saving his life and defeating the book's villains. Horrified to have found himself unwittingly complicit in the arrest of Kit and dismayed in the face of the oppression of the little girl in the Brasses' cellar, Swiveller comes to realize that casual amusement is an inadequate response to the world about him, and his interest in these two leads to his active engagement on their behalf. It was significant for Dickens's artistry that Swiveller's curiosity stimulates his moral growth, in the author's first depiction of what was to become a central axiom of his art—namely, the ethical power of imagination, which, Dickens showed, had the capacity to be a vital force for good in a wicked world.

The other story, which took over the miscellaneous conception of *Master Humphrey's Clock*, was *Barnaby Rudge*. Under its earlier title, *Gabriel Varden*, it was a work of long gestation and the first of

Dickens's books to realize his conception of what a modern novel should be: namely, following the massive achievement of Sir Walter Scott, a tale that placed fictional characters in actual historical events from the recent past. Scott located his Scottish novels in flashpoints of history, in which an accommodation of romantic Scotland to English practicality was effected; Barnaby Rudge looked back to the Gordon riots of 1780 when religious controversy erupted violently under the "No Popery" banner of the rioters. Just as Scott's historical imagination allowed him to confront pressing issues of nationalism in his day, so too Dickens's subject had parallels with the tensions epitomized by the Catholic emancipation act of 1829. But while Scott embraced an essentially progressive Whig view of history, Dickens's vision was apocalyptic, conceiving history as the gradual building of tensions until they explode in violence, after which the process repeats itself over and over again.

The story's protagonist, a Scott-like wise fool, was placed in a mixture of mystery, murder, and romance. Barnaby's alter ego, a raven named Grip, so tickled Dickens's fancy that he adopted a raven of his own as a pet. Dolly Vardon [the spelling of the surname altered along the way] quickly established herself as Dickens's most popular non-tragic heroine, and the surly Hugh cut a haunting figure. The emotional core of the book—what Dickens described as "the attraction of repulsion"—was the lurid depiction of the rioting, led by a hangman, a half-wit, and an alienated bastard. Most importantly, the challenge of meeting his most famous predecessor on his own ground freed Dickens to move on to a new, highly individual kind of fiction: whereas his first works owed more to literary precedent than to innovation, the novels which followed broke new ground in conception, style, and organization; hereafter, Dickens's novels became more important in the course of literary history for the precedents they set than for what they inherited from the past.

With the completion of Barnaby Rudge, Dickens took the first extended break from writing, but even the setbacks of Bentley's Miscellany and Master Humphrey's Clock failed to dampen his hankering for journalism. Over the next decade, he wrote a stream of articles—mainly theater reviews and letters to newspaper editors—and for a few weeks, he undertook the role of editor for a newspaper, the *Daily News*, which began publication in January 1846. Dickens hired staff and saw the first issues go to press, but after only a fortnight found himself wholly unsuited for the humdrum chore of running a daily paper, and resigned.

4. Dickens the Traveler

From the time of Dickens's first sketches, newspapers were saturated with notices, reviews, reprints, and excerpts of his works, and the heavyweight cultural journals weighed in with discussions of his unprecedented popularity. Dramatizations and imitations were everywhere. *Pickwick* was evergreen, and sales of the final installments of *The Old Curiosity Shop* reached 100,000 copies a week. Dickens's prowess as a public speaker put him in increasing demand for the rest of his life. In 1841, not yet 30 years old, he was invited to a banquet in his honor in Edinburgh, where he was given the Freedom of the City award, a distinction traditionally bestowed on more senior members of the community.

Great as these accolades were, nothing could have prepared Dickens for the reception he received while traveling with Catherine through North America the next year. After five years of non-stop writing he needed a break and, promising to write a travel book based on his visit, he convinced Chapman and Hall to subsidize a trip to the New World. After a harrowing crossing of the Atlantic, he and Catherine arrived in Boston, shouting, as they entered the Tremont House Hotel, "Here we are!"—a catchphrase coined by Joseph Grimaldi, the clown whose memoirs Dickens edited in 1838. In an era before the advent of the celebrity culture so commonplace today, Dickens had made no provision for handlers and had not even hired an assistant to deal with arrangements (an omission quickly remedied by the appointment of George Washington Putnam as his secretary). Still, his fame preceded him and Dickens was greeted frenetically. Crowds followed him wherever he went; people queued up for hours to shake his hand; newspapers clamored for details of his every move; delegations invited him to dinners, receptions, and parties. At the Park Theater in New York, 3,000 admirers crowded in for a "Boz Ball," while another 5,000 who were unable to obtain tickets, milled outside in the hope of getting a glimpse of the English author. He was introduced to the foremost American literati—Washington Irving, Edgar Allan Poe, James Russell Lowell, Oliver Wendell Holmes, Henry Wadsworth Longfellow, and Cornelius Conway Felton—some of whom became his lifelong friends. He was even granted an audience with John Tyler, President of the United States.

Dickens's initial reaction was delight. "It is impossible to tell you what a reception I have had here," he wrote to Macready. "They cheer me in the Theatres; in the streets; within doors; and without . . . Americans . . . are as delicate, as considerate, as careful of giving the least offense, as the best Englishmen I ever saw.—I like their behaviour to Ladies infinitely better than that of my own countrymen; and their Institutions I reverence, love and honor." But his view changed fundamentally in a matter of days, as Dickens became more familiar with some of the habits and behaviors of the American public. For instance, he was appalled by the ubiquitous practice of spitting while chewing tobacco. He found Americans' lack of personal hygiene offensive. He thought that people were pushy, ignorant, opinionated, and self-important. And he complained that railway carriages were grossly overheated. Astonishingly, England's great humorist did not understand the distinctly American idiom of the "tall tale;" he thought people were trying to deceive him when their anecdotes became outlandish. Above all, Dickens found the institution of slavery deeply disturbing. But the issue that really outraged him was the unfairness of international copyright laws. To Dickens, the common practice of not remunerating writers for works published outside their own countries was not merely a matter of self-interest, but of justice as well. When he spoke about it, he was greeted with scurrilous personal attacks in the press—a reaction which prompted Dickens to redouble the challenge: everywhere he went, he decried the unjust copyright system. As he pointed out, it affected American writers every bit as much as it did English authors like himself. This was not a popular issue to speak about, so even friends who agreed with Dickens's stance cautioned silence, which merely made him more determined to continue speaking out, even in the face of growing criticism.

From New York, Dickens traveled to Philadelphia, and then Washington and Richmond, declining to proceed further south to slave states. He then turned west, proceeding to Pittsburgh, Cincinnati and Louisville, eventually reaching the junction of the Ohio and Mississippi rivers and St. Louis, before going to the Great Lakes and Niagara Falls. The raw, undeveloped state of what was still the frontier appalled him, and he found Looking Glass Prairie near St. Louis to be less impressive than Salisbury Plain, a scenic plateau in southern England. And although Dickens was awe-struck by Niagara Falls, he found it less spectacular than Glencoe in the Scottish Highlands. From Niagara, he crossed over into Canada, where he immersed himself in theatricals in Montreal, before returning to England in June.

Dickens's over-riding reaction to his North American visit was disappointment. "This is not the Republic I came to see," he confided to Macready. "This is not the Republic of my imagination." Mark Tapley, a character in Dickens's 1843 novel *Martin Chuzzlewit*, summed up the author's own impression of the New World. Explaining how he would paint the bald eagle, a symbol of America, Tapley said: "I should draw it like a Bat, for its short-sightedness; like a Bantam, for its bragging; like a Magpie, for its honesty; like a Peacock, for its vanity; like an Ostrich, for its putting its head in the mud, and thinking nobody sees it." The book's eponymous protagonist went even further, adding that the eagle could also be depicted "like a Phoenix, for its power of springing from the ashes of its faults and vices, and soaring up anew into the sky." What Dickens discovered during his trip was the complexity of being a popular writer, and, above all, just how quintessentially English he was.

While in America, Dickens wrote long, circumstantial letters to friends back home, which brimmed with lively, spontaneous impressions of everything he saw and everyone he met. He drew on these reports extensively when writing his travelogue, *American Notes for General Circulation* (published in 1842), but excised much of the personal flavor of the letters, omitting discussion of the reception he was accorded, toning down comments on individuals, and largely avoiding the imaginative liveliness that made his writing elsewhere so vividly engaging. Instead, he focused mainly on institutions he inspected and places he visited and lifted from other writers verbatim accounts of Laura Bridgman, the deaf and blind girl he met, and an attack on slavery. In *American Notes*, Dickens also pointed to the unreliability of the country's paper currency and the expected pirating of the book in America.

Predictably, the response in America was hostile, but British reviewers were also less than enthusiastic. They found Dickens's account to be a little more than a rehash of the reactions of earlier British visitors to America, such as English novelist Frances Trollope, and thought it lacked depth or vitality. Uncharacteristically, Dickens had written a dull book. However, he more than made up for it in the American episodes of *Martin Chuzzlewit*, in which Martin and Mark go to America in hope of making their fortune. Martin experiences the absurdities of lionizing that Dickens himself had endured, and the American characters are among the most hilariously satiric vignettes Dickens ever wrote: among them Mrs. Hominy, the Mother of the Modern Gracchi; Jefferson Brick, the war correspondent for the New York Rowdy Journal; and Hannibal Chollop, whose "bright home is in the settin Sun." Martin's land speculation turns out to be a fetid swamp, in which both he and Mark nearly die of fever, and they flee back to England chastened, as Dickens had been, by their experience.

For all his fame, however, Dickens had not managed to achieve financial security, and with a growing family to provide for, he was determined to save money by moving abroad for a year. In July 1844, he rented an enormous coach, which lumbered with a party of 12 across France and into Italy, stopping finally in Genoa. From this base, he toured Italy and wrote *The Chimes*. He dashed back to London in December to read this Christmas book to select groups of friends. On his return journey, he stopped in Paris, where he met a number of eminent French writers. In the new year, he and

Catherine made a second tour of Italy, including a memorable ascent of Mount Vesuvius. Notable events during his stay in Genoa were a vivid dream of his late sister-in-law Mary Hogarth, in which—bizarrely—she urged him to convert to Roman Catholicism, as well as an extended attempt (which fascinated Dickens but roused Catherine's jealousy) to cure, by mesmerism, the wife of an English acquaintance, Augusta de la Rue, who suffered from a nervous disorder.

The stay in Genoa formed the basis of a series of *Travelling Letters*, which described his impressions of Italy and were published in the *Daily News* in 1846; they were subsequently gathered, revised, and supplemented in a second travel book, *Pictures from Italy*. Unlike his previous volume, this work embraced an imaginative vision, referring to his method as "reflections" or "mere shadows in the water," in which people and places were explicitly viewed as though in a dreamlike state. The emphasis was on spectacle and spectators—with Dickens both the observer and the observed, as peasants gathered round to view the English tourists and beg. He disavowed any concern with history or politics, despite the fact that he had strong and lasting views on the revolutionary turmoil that convulsed Italy at the time. His focus was not on classical Rome, but on contemporary Italy, in which he found the ubiquitous juxtaposition of grand beauty and abject poverty; he pointed his finger firmly at the Roman Catholic Church, for what he saw as the flummery of its theatrical rituals, as well as for its role in condemning people to deprivation and superstition. The book's first illustrator, Dickens's friend Clarkson Stanfield (himself a Catholic) resigned from the collaboration on account of these outspoken religious views.

Pictures from Italy marked a return to the genial narrative voice of *Sketches by Boz*. Descriptions, such as the puppet show—"the drollest exhibition I ever beheld in my life"—and Vesuvius "spouting fire," have a vividness quite lacking anywhere in *American Notes*. And Italy retained its attraction for Dickens; he returned there with the English novelist Wilkie Collins and the artist Augustus Egg in 1853.

He published a stream of articles on the political ferment there in *Household Words* and *All the Year Round*; in *David Copperfield*, Little Emily flees to a village near Naples, and in *Little Dorrit* the Dorrit entourage travels to Venice and Rome, where William Dorrit has the stroke which kills him.

Leaving Italy in June 1845, Dickens returned with his family to London, where he was soon wholly engrossed in an amateur theatrical production of Ben Jonson's *Every Man in His Humour*, for which he was the producer, director, and leading actor. There was even a private performance for Queen Victoria and Prince Albert. But he was not yet finished with his travels: after a brief engagement with the *Daily News*, Dickens took his family to Switzerland. They resided in Lausanne for the next six months, where he wrote the first chapters of *Dombey and Son*. He found the rural setting on Lake Geneva a mixed blessing. An inveterate walker, he relied on the crowded streets of London for inspiration, and found their absence crippling: "The toil and labour of writing, day after day, without that magic lantern, is IMMENSE!!" he told Forster. But he considered the Alps and, above all, the Convent of the Great St. Bernard, "most extraordinary" and certainly inspirational: David Copperfield sought Wordsworthian solace in the Alps after Dora's death; the murderous conflict between Vendale and Obenreizer in *No Thoroughfare* was set in the inhospitable mountains, and the Dorrits spent the night in the Convent on their way to Italy. Dickens dedicated *The Battle of Life*, his Christmas book of that year, to "my English friends in Switzerland," and his next novel, *David Copperfield*, to other close friends he made there, Richard and Lavinia Watson.

But of all Dickens's travels, the country he visited most and felt the greatest kinship with was France. His first visit was to Calais with Catherine and his illustrator Hablot Browne for a few days in July 1837, when he was enthralled by the gaiety and egalitarianism of the French. He passed through France again on his way to Italy in 1844 and enjoyed the first of many visits to Paris. Later, he took family holidays in Boulogne, where he found a congenial writing environment—large parts of *Bleak House*, *Hard Times* and *Little Dorrit* were composed there. He also made friends with his landlord, Ferdinand Beaucourt-Mutuel, a man of "a highly convivial temperament, and his hospitality is unbounded."

In one of Dickens's *Household Words* sketches, "Some Account of an Extraordinary Traveller," the traveler, Mr. Booley, took trips all over the world without ever leaving London. He accomplished this simply by looking at large, lifelike paintings called "panoramas," which were popular in Victorian times. Dickens himself made imaginary journeys to places where he never set foot and, in this sense, he traveled beyond Europe and North America. The Anglo-Bengalee Disinterested Loan and Life Assurance Company in *Martin Chuzzlewit* owed its name to the East India Company; in *Dombey and Son*, Major Bagstock, who had served in India and cultivated a penchant for strong curries, had an Indian servant, known only as the Native. In *David Copperfield*, the Micawbers and Peggottys emigrated to Australia, and in *Great Expectations*, the convict Magwitch returned from penal transportation there. Dickens himself seriously considered undertaking a reading tour of Australia, and later sent two of his sons, Alfred and Plorn, to settle there. And in his last, unfinished novel, *The Mystery of Edwin Drood*, the twins Neville and Helena Landless had come from Ceylon.

5. Memory and Growth: Dickens in the 1840s

In the decade following the shock of his American experience, Dickens undertook a searching revaluation of his role as a popular author, clarifying his central beliefs and introducing radical innovation in his artistry. Although never one for passively adapting traditions he inherited, and only rarely reprising materials he had previously used, the 1840s marked a radical shift of gears, as he achieved new levels of complexity and excellence in his craft. This stock-taking involved painful meditation on events from his past, a coming to terms with the hardships and frustrations he had undergone, and—if not an exorcism of his demons—at least a new ability to draw on his past with consummate creativity.

Martin Chuzzlewit, the novel he wrote after his return from North America, marked a new beginning in several ways. Focusing on a variety of manifestations of selfishness, *Chuzzlewit* was the first of his novels to place thematic unity at its core. With all of the characters, both in England and North America, Dickens worked, for the first time, variations on a central motif, making it a structural principle. We have already seen how he introduced an array of American characters, each defined by narrow-minded, prejudiced egotism; similarly, all of the Chuzzlewit clan were motivated by self-aggrandizement: Mrs. Gamp was cocooned in a solipsistic world of her own; Mr. Pecksniff thrived complacently in an utterly specious self-image as a moral exemplar; and even poor Tom Pinch—a prime instance of critic and novelist Chesterton's observation that Dickens had a tendency to treat his characters as guests—was marked by his complete *lack* of self-interest.

Young Martin represented another departure for Dickens—a character whose moral growth was central to the author's conception. Previous protagonists—Oliver, Nell, Barnaby—utterly lacked inner development; Mr. Pickwick was minimally defined by the education he received from Sam Weller and his incarceration in the Fleet Prison, and even Nicholas Nickleby experienced only perfunctory growth in worldly wisdom as a result of his adventures. Oliver and Nell were both static embodiments of the "principle of good" (as Dickens described Oliver in his Preface), and Barnaby's addled brain left him incapable of development. But young Martin, who started out impervious to the feelings of others, learned from his experience in Eden to look beyond his personal concerns. His moral development was scarcely one of Dickens's great achievements, but it pointed the way to a new concern with the evolving inner lives of his characters, which distinguished all of Dickens's later fiction.

On the other hand, the book's triumph rested on two characters who were quite impervious to change. William Hazlitt, writing a generation before Dickens and thinking of Don Quixote, suggested that a particularly rich vein of comedy occurred in "consistency in absurdity;" a method, which he called "keeping in comic character." "That reason and good sense," he wrote, "should be consistent, is not wonderful: but that caprice, and whim, and fantastical prejudice, should be uniform and infallible in their results, is the surprising thing." This description accurately identified the source of hilarity aroused by the characterizations of Pecksniff and Gamp, and later of Mr. Micawber and Flora Finching. Dickens delighted in placing Pecksniff's absurd urbanity in situations where it seemed impossible for the character not to be flustered. In chapter 20, for example, the monthly part ended with old Martin (whom Pecksniff was trying to bilk) arriving at Pecksniff's door, at just the moment when the house was in chaos because Jonas Chuzzlewit had proposed to the wrong daughter. By switching in the next serial number to events in North America, Dickens kept first readers on the edge of their seats for two whole months, wondering how Pecksniff coped. Again, in the story's conclusion, when his rascality was publicly exposed, Pecksniff reacted by forgiving old Martin for knocking him down. Mrs. Gamp, likewise, buttressed her own comfort by incessantly quoting paeans of praise from her imaginary friend and admirer Mrs. Harris, and she rose magnificently from the shock of Betsy Prig's apostasy: when her crony announced that she 'don't believe there's no sich a person!' Mrs. Gamp solemnly responded:

> "Wot I have took from Betsey Prig this blessed night, no mortial creetur knows! If she had abuged me, bein' in liquor, which I thought I smelt her wen she come, but could not so believe, not bein' used myself"—Mrs Gamp, by the way, was pretty far gone, and the fragrance of the teapot [filled with gin] was strong in the room—"I could have bore it with a thankful art. But the words she spoke of Mrs Harris, lambs could not forgive. No, Betsey!" said Mrs Gamp, in a violent burst of feeling, "nor worms forget!"

Dickens was confident that *Chuzzlewit* was "in a hundred points immeasurably the best of my stories," but sales were poor—whether from his extended absence from public view, the economic hardship in the country, or some other possible causes. When his publisher William Hall ill-advisedly hinted that the author might, in consequence, have to take a pay-cut, Dickens became furious, and resolved to break away from the firm he had not long previously described as "the best of booksellers past, present, or to come." He initiated a new arrangement with Bradbury and Evans, who had up to then worked as printers only, and made a lucrative contract with them. His determination to change publishers was reinforced when the sumptuous production of *A Christmas Carol* that winter, with color plates and gold embossing, meant that despite vigorous sales, profits from that work were much lower than he anticipated.

Dickens interrupted work on *Chuzzlewit* to write the *Carol*, which, upon its publication in December 1843, immediately became one of his best-loved works, endlessly reprinted and adapted. Although he had written about the festive season previously, in one of the *Sketches by Boz*, and again in the "Story of the Goblins Who Stole Christmas" (one of the inset tales in *Pickwick*), it was the *Carol* that had irrevocably established his association with Christmas in the public mind. It is the best work he ever wrote: comic, pathetic, hard-hitting, simultaneously fanciful, realistic, and perfectly poised in structure and tone. It dramatizes the joys of cheerful conviviality and encapsulates the central pillar of his philosophy, which is the necessity of selfless fellow feeling. This little book also marks a crucial development in Dickens's thinking: a growing conviction that by facing the sorrows and hardships of one's past, a person gains self-understanding. When the miser Scrooge is taken back by the first of the three spirits to his own lonely boyhood, the tears he sheds on seeing his former self, cleanses his soul and, by teaching him the value of love for others, brings him happiness. Wisdom and maturity, Dickens shows, depend on a living sense of one's own past. He encapsulated that belief in the motto of one of his later Christmas books, *The Haunted Man*, in which he wrote, "Lord keep my memory green."

After the *Carol*, Dickens wrote four more Christmas books: *The Chimes* (1844), *The Cricket on the Hearth* (1845), *The Battle of Life* (1846), and the above-mentioned *The Haunted Man* (1848). These books consolidated the association of Dickens's name with Christmas and evolved into the Christmas stories, an annual feature of his periodicals, a special issue containing a series of short stories by several authors, written for (rather than about) Christmas, in a framework devised by Dickens. While the *Carol* was both for and about Christmas, the later Christmas books and stories were tales *for* Christmas only, and none captured the celebratory mood so exquisitely as the depiction of Fezziwig's ball, the dinner at the Cratchits, and games at the house of Scrooge's nephew. For Dickens's readers, these later works did not evoke the meaning of Yuletide quite as emphatically as the *Carol* did.

Following his sojourn in Italy, and his brief stint as editor of the *Daily News*, Dickens returned to Switzerland, where he began work on *Dombey and Son*, generally seen as the commencement of his full maturity as a novelist. Like *Chuzzlewit*, it is centered on a "leading idea," but while *Chuzzlewit* simply worked variations on a theme, *Dombey* was the first of Dickens's novels to be governed by a narrative structure, which developed a strong, overarching theme—in this case, pride. Not coincidentally, it was also the first of Dickens's novels for which detailed working notes setting forth his plans for the entire book have survived to this day. The full title of the work pointed to its purpose: *Dealings with the Firm of Dombey and Son, Wholesale, Retail, and for Exportation*. Dickens was concerned with dramatizing the consequences of trying to organize one's personal life along business principles, and the novel showed the results to be disastrous. The story begins with Mr. Dombey welcoming his newborn son, Paul, into the world as the heir to the firm of Dombey and Son. When, a quarter of the way into the tale, Paul dies, Dombey sets out to find a new wife (the previous one having died during childbirth)—not as a companion, but as a functional necessity for the production of a new heir. The collapse of that marriage signals the ruin of Dombey's business, and it is left to his daughter Florence, who was neglected and abused from the start, to nurture him back to life on a new, domestic basis.

The novel was vigorously engaged with one of the principal industrial events of the day, namely, the coming of the railway. In the decade and a half since the opening of the Liverpool and Manchester Railway in 1830, over 1500 miles of track had been laid in the United Kingdom, and an extra 2500 miles sanctioned. The speed, noise, smoke, and upheaval—vividly evoked in Dickens's description of Staggs's Gardens—made the railway a vivid symbol of the radical physical, social, economic, and psychological transformation. As Kathleen Tillotson, one of the most distinguished Victorian scholars pointed out, *Dombey* was the first of Dickens's novels to confront social issues not as specific, remediable wrongs, but with "a pervasive unease" about the very fabric of society. The railway brought new prosperity to the Toodles family, but it also precipitated Carker's violent death.

In this novel, the mercantile themes are interwoven with gender issues, both erotic and filial. The subplot dealing with the prostitute Alice Marwood is explicitly sexual, but Carker's attempted seduction of Edith Dombey owes more to his rivalry with his employer than to sex. Far more important is the contrast between nurturing femininity—introduced in the person of Polly Toodle, hired as wet nurse to keep the infant Paul alive—and the male energies represented by Mr. Dombey. In the final reconciliation of Dombey with Florence, she places his head gently upon her breast—the very breast, which, in frustrated outrage, he had previously struck and bruised. In Dickens's mind, feminine values are important for humanity. They are seen most overtly in the love of little Paul and Florence, and more complexly in the relationship between Florence and Edith. Men such as Walter Gay and Sol Gills share these values, whereas their absence is depicted in "good" Mrs. Brown, in Mrs. Chick, and in Mrs. Skewton.

Dickens articulated these values in a delicate balance between realism and fairy tale. The latter is evident not only in the miraculous survival of Walter Gay and the happy reconciliation of father and daughter—and the dog, which Dickens remembered at the last minute to include in the finale—but also in the character of the ogress Mrs. Pipchin. The latter was drawn from the real life Dickens told Forster, recollecting his landlady in the blacking warehouse days. Memories of his childhood inspired one of the book's triumphs—the depiction of Paul's final days as seen through his own eyes. Whereas Dickens had invited us to look *at* Little Nell's sufferings, with Paul we look *through* the child's vision as his life ebbed away. Famously, Dickens's fellow novelist William Makepeace Thackeray, at work on his masterpiece *Vanity Fair* at the time, read the chapter presenting Paul's death and exclaimed, "There's no writing against such power as this—one has no chance . . . it is unsurpassed—it is stupendous."

At some point during those years, Dickens began to write an autobiography. He wrote happily about his childhood in Chatham, anxiously about his father's financial troubles, and bravely about his own employment in the blacking warehouse, but when he came to recall his failed romance with Maria Beadnell, he abandoned the project. He gave the unfinished manuscript to Forster, who preserved it and reprinted portions of it in his *Life*, published two years after Dickens's death. There for the first time Dickens's public, and even his friends and closest family, learned of his employment in the blacking warehouse and discovered the source of his growing conviction about the importance of facing one's past. The significance of Dickens's attempt at penning his autobiography cannot be overstated: not only because his experiences offered the key to essential traits of his character—a deeply mixed attitude to his parents, shyness in close relationships, profound insecurity about his social respectability, terror of financial failure, and iron determination to succeed—but also due to his belief that facing and overcoming hardships tempered the character.

Several momentous results followed directly from this retrospection and revaluation to which the autobiographical fragment attests. The first was a return to Dickens's earlier ambition to edit a periodical miscellany. Secondly, he wanted to give public readings from his works. The third was a project to publish an inexpensive collected edition of his works. An explicit statement of the vital importance of facing one's sorrows, as exemplified in *The Haunted Man*, followed. And finally, on Forster's suggestion, a decision to transform Dickens's unfinished autobiography into a fictionalized account of his childhood and adolescence in a first-person narration took shape.

What happened to all these plans? Despite the setbacks he suffered while editing *Bentley's Miscellany*, *Master Humphrey's Clock*, and the *Daily News*, Dickens continued to aspire to conduct a periodical journal. In 1845, he wrote to Forster, outlining the idea for a weekly miscellany to be called *The Cricket*: "*Carol* philosophy, cheerful views, sharp anatomization of humbug, jolly good temper, papers always in season, pat to the time of year; and a vein of glowing, hearty, generous, mirthful, beaming reference to everything to Home, and Fireside." Nothing came of this idea, save the title for that year's Christmas book, *The Cricket on the Hearth*. Four years later, he tried again with a revised proposal for a periodical, this time, to be organized around the idea of a "cheerful, useful, and always welcome Shadow." Once more, the idea was for a weekly miscellany, partly original, partly select, with emphasis on variety. As before, nothing came of it until 1850, when he finally launched *Household Words*, which continued, with a modulation into *All the Year Round* in 1859, until long after Dickens's death.

Regarding his second plan, it was during the writing of *Dombey* that Dickens first proposed giving public readings of his works. "I was thinking the other day," he wrote to Forster, "that in these days of lecturings and readings, a great deal of money might possibly be made (if it were not infra dig) by one's having Readings of one's own books." Forster's verdict was that the idea was decidedly "infra dig" (i.e. undignified), and Dickens set the notion aside for more than a decade. He had, however, from the very start of his career read from his writings to family and friends; he raced back from Italy in 1844 to read *The Chimes* to a select group, and although he did not commence public readings for his own profit until 1858, on several occasions during the 1850s, he gave readings from his works for charitable causes.

Dickens's third ambition was realized, between 1847 and 1850, when Chapman and Hall brought out a uniform edition of his works, in an inexpensive, double-column format without illustrations. Dickens wrote new prefaces, in some of which he looked back on his career up to that point. For example, in the Preface to *Sketches by Boz*, which was the source of great pride on its initial appearance, he described the tales as mere apprentice work, "extremely crude and ill-considered." Many of today's readers and literary critics disagree with this verdict, but it is a clear indication of the extent to which Dickens's artistic ambitions had developed. In another of the Cheap Edition prefaces, he made a spirited claim for the realism of his writing, much as he was later to do in defense of Krook's death by spontaneous combustion in *Bleak House*, and Blandois's death in the falling house in *Little Dorrit*. In light of the decline of his reputation in the later decades of the 19th century (the heyday of literary realism)—and for that matter, one of the primary bases of the revival of that reputation in the later decades of the 1900s (the heyday of magical realism)—it is interesting to note Forster's claim, in his *Life of Charles Dickens*, of "his indifference to any praise of his performances on the merely literary side, compared with the higher recognition of them as bits of actual life, with the meaning and purpose on their part, and the responsibility on his, of realities rather than creatures of fancy." That view needs to be qualified by another statement by Dickens, also recorded by Forster, which takes us to the core of Dickens's artistry:

> It does not seem to me to be enough to say of any description that it is the exact truth. The exact truth must be there; but the merit or art in the narrator, is the manner of stating the truth. As to which thing in literature, it always seems to me that there is a world to be done. And in these times, when the tendency is to be frightfully literal and catalogue-like—to make the thing, in short, a sort of sum in reduction that any miserable creature can do in that way—I have an idea (really founded on the love of what I profess), that the very holding of popular literature through a kind of popular dark age, may depend on such fanciful treatment.

Dickens's most overt statement about the importance of looking back is to be found in his fifth and final Christmas book, written and published in 1848. *The Haunted Man* is the story of a chemist named Redlaw, who was embittered by sorrows from his past. One Christmas Eve offered a wish by his ghostly double, he asked for forgetfulness, only to discover that the loss of unhappy memories compromised his capacity for compassion. While discovering the importance of remembering sadness as well as joys from the past, he asked for the wish to be rescinded, upon which his human feeling was restored. While not the best of Dickens's stories, it nevertheless expressed with particular clarity his conviction of the beneficent power of memory, and the necessity of facing hardships and unhappiness squarely.

The culminating retrospection of the decade of the 1840s, however, was *David Copperfield*. In this book, Dickens drew upon his own past more directly than anywhere else in his published writing, in places simply transposing his own experiences into David's life. Dickens's own happy childhood at Ordnance Terrace was transformed into David's communion with Peggotty; his sense of abandonment by his parents was reflected in the death of David's father and his mother's remarriage. Warrens' Blacking became Murdstone and Grinby, and his unrequited love affair with Maria Beadnell formed the basis for David's love for Dora Spenlow. Like Dickens in his youth, David too struggled to learn shorthand and acquired a hearty contempt for Doctors' Commons, before, by dint of hard work, gaining success as a novelist. The impecunious Mr. Micawber, waiting endlessly for something to turn up, was a comic embodiment of Dickens's own father, for whom he eventually came to have a deep love and respect. The first-person narration, deployed for the first time by Dickens, brought intimacy and authenticity to the novel, along with a vivid sense of his personal engagement with the adventures.

But the novel is much more than merely a fictionalized retelling of Dickens's own life story. Although less focused on social issues than any of his other novels, *Copperfield* raises many thematic issues through its large cast of characters and intricate structural parallelism, as Dickens worked variations through the multiple strands of the narrative. Thus, David's endeavor to form Dora's character echoed Murdstone's manipulation of David's mother. David's courtship of Dora was counterpointed by Traddles's love for his Sophy, and David's aspirations were thrown into perspective by Uriah Heep's efforts not only to succeed in business, but also to marry Agnes. Steerforth's seduction of Little Em'ly indicated a possible outcome of Annie Strong's attraction to Jack Maldon. In these and other parallels, Dickens worked rich variations on character and situation.

David Copperfield is, furthermore, a novel closely attuned to the spirit of the age in which it was written. In the book's opening sentence, David wondered whether he would turn out to be the hero of his own story, drawing on the conception of "heroism"–not as military glory, but as evidenced in the man of letters, proposed in

Thomas Carlyle's classic study, *On Heroes and Hero Worship* (1841). Just months before Dickens began *Copperfield*, Charlotte Brontë's *Jane Eyre*, the story of an adolescent passing through love tests to maturity, was published. Even as Dickens's novel was appearing in serial parts, the two foremost poems of the century were released: (like *Jane Eyre*, written in first-person narratives) William Wordsworth's *Prelude*, the great Romantic poem on personal growth achieved through communion with nature, and Alfred Lord Tennyson's *In Memoriam*, reclaiming values in the face of devastating loss. David, confronted with the death of Dora, retreated to the Alps, where he took stock of his emotions as well as personal and spiritual values.

Finally, and most importantly, despite being focused on David's passage from childhood through adolescence to adulthood, Dickens was less concerned with his hero's growth to maturity than with his cherishing of memory. In the course of his adventures, David learned how to manage his undisciplined heart, but the overwhelming momentum of the book is with the preservation of the memories and values of childhood. Thus, David found in Dora, a reincarnation of his mother's immature charm; he cherished in the Micawbers not irresponsibility and fecklessness, but gaiety and optimism; his final vision of Steerforth was not of the destroyer of Em'ly, Ham, and Mr. Peggotty, but of the schoolmate who befriended him when he was lonely. Dickens considered *David Copperfield* his "favourite child," a verdict widely shared. His achievement was less of *Bildungsroman*—a novel of personal growth—than a glorious retrospection, clinging to memory to the lost joys of childhood.

6. Dickens as Editor – Continued

As we have seen, Dickens aspired to edit a miscellaneous periodical from very early in his career. With the commencement of *Household Words* in 1850, he triumphantly achieved that goal. The weekly magazine quickly established a large, steady circulation of nearly 40,000 copies per issue—increasing to around 80,000 for the popular Christmas editions. And, with a change of title and direction in the disruptive circumstances of his marital break-up in 1858, it continued publication until 1895, long after Dickens's death.

The very first article in the inaugural issue, "A Preliminary Word," (March 30, 1850), spelled out his intentions for the journal: to present "knowledge . . . from the stirring world around us, [conveyed in] "no mere utilitarian spirit." Instead, Dickens promised, his journal would endeavor to "cherish that light of Fancy which is inherent in the human breast; which . . . can never be extinguished." Centrally, the "Preliminary Word" articulated this axiom, dear to his heart and central to his goals for the magazine: "One main object of our Household Words," he declared, was "to show to all, that in all familiar things, even in those which are repellent on the surface, there is Romance enough, if we will find it out." He repeated this injunction (in capital letters) in a memo to his sub-editor three years later: "KEEP 'HOUSEHOLD WORDS' IMAGINATIVE is the solemn and continual conductorial injunction." An identical sentiment was to appear in the Preface to his next novel: "In *Bleak House*," he wrote, "I have purposely dwelt upon the romantic side of familiar things." And in the novel after that, *Hard Times*, the story depicted the disastrous consequences of Mr. Gradgrind's attempt to root out the fancy "inherent in the human breast" from his daughter Louisa. Imagination, or "fancy," as he preferred to call it, was arguably the single most important tenet of Dickens's vision, first fully articulated (as we have seen) in the character of Dick Swiveller in *The Old Curiosity Shop*, and repeatedly invoked ever after.

Dickens's intention was a direct challenge to the established inexpensive weekly *Chambers's Journal*, which he found "as congenial to me, generally, as the brown paper packages in which ironmongers keep Nails." He also aimed to distance *Household Words* from the best-selling radical and sensationalist *Reynold's Weekly Newspaper*, whose publishers he described (with reference to the excesses of the French Revolution) as the "Bastards of the Mountain, draggled fringe of the Red Cap, Panders to the basest passions of the lowest natures."

Dickens took the title of his new enterprise from Shakespeare's *Henry V*, the scene in which Henry declared to each survivor of the battle of Agincourt that the names of the heroes there would be "as familiar in his mouth as household words" (act 4, scene 3). Articles in the journal were anonymous, but each page opening was headed with the notice, "Conducted by Charles Dickens," which, as his friend Douglas Jerrold (who declined to contribute) quipped, made the journal "mononymous." By maintaining close editorial control and writing many articles himself, Dickens ensured that the magazine sustained a basic homogeneity of tone and outlook, presented as his own. His claim in 1853 that he had read 900 unsolicited manuscripts submitted over the previous year, from which—after extensive revision by himself—just 11 were published, showed the extent of the control Dickens maintained over his publication.

The office book, which has survived and has been reproduced with copious annotation in a volume edited by Anne Lohrli, provides detailed information about the journal. Over its 10-year publication, nearly 400 writers contributed to its pages, including several well-known figures such as Elizabeth Gaskell and Wilkie Collins. Dickens recruited an editorial staff, headed by his sub-editor W. H. Wills, who contributed a significant portion of the journal's contents. Dickens himself was a prolific contributor, writing over 100 full-length pieces himself, co-authoring many others, suggesting subjects for articles, and generally keeping tight editorial control over the entire contents.

From the outset, *Household Words* maintained the miscellaneous character Dickens sought. Approximately a third of the articles were literary entertainment; there was biography and history, social commentary, satire on contemporary issues, and surveys of London life. The publication also consisted of poetry, humorous squibs, and what he referred to as "process" articles, which explained how something was manufactured or developed in nature. The densely printed 24 double-column pages of each weekly issue were supplemented for five years by a monthly news digest entitled *Household Narrative of Current Events*. Initially, *Household Words* did not include serial fiction, until a dip in sales led Dickens to write *Hard Times* as the lead entry for 20 weeks in 1854. It is ironic that Dickens's satiric attack on hard-headed utilitarian outlook was motivated by strict business calculations. By far the shortest of Dickens's novels, *Hard Times* succeeded handsomely in its commercial intention, increasing sales of the journal four- or five-fold.

Dickens personally held 50 percent ownership of *Household Words* and paid himself a salary of £500 per year, plus payment for his own contributions. Bradbury and Evans, the publishers, had 25 percent ownership; Wills and Forster 12 ½ percent each. That arrangement came abruptly to an end when Dickens quarreled with Bradbury and Evans in 1858 over their refusal to print his personal statement about the breakup of his marriage in *Punch*, the humorous magazine, which they also published. Dickens dissolved the partnership and terminated publication of *Household Words*, founding a new weekly periodical in its stead, *All the Year Round*. In the arrangements for the new title, Dickens owned 75 percent of the magazine, while Wills owned the other 25 percent. In effect, Dickens became his own publisher.

Like its predecessor, *All the Year Round* took its title from Shakespeare, adapting a quotation from *Othello*, "the story of my life

/ From year to year," but only after Dickens reluctantly accepted Forster's observation that his originally proposed notion, "Household Harmony," was, under the circumstances, signally inappropriate. Also, like the previous periodical, *All the Year Round* was a weekly miscellany, but it differed in essential ways from the start.

First, each issue opened with a serial novel. The opening number got the project off to a rousing start: "It was the best of times, it was the worst of times," and when *A Tale of Two Cities* concluded 35 weeks later, the work that succeeded it was hardly less successful: Wilkie Collins's sensation novel *The Woman in White*. The periodical reached weekly sales of 125,000, a figure that was tripled when Collins's *The Moonstone* took over as the lead serial. Sales were dependent on the attractiveness of the current novel, and when Charles Lever's *A Day's Ride* failed to maintain readership, Dickens had to replace it as the opening entry with his own *Great Expectations*, quickly restructured from a 20-part monthly serial to a shorter, weekly publication. As in the case of *Household Words*, the extra Christmas issues of *All the Year Round* enjoyed unique popularity, selling 300,000 copies. Moreover, sales in the United States were even more phenomenal, estimated at a circulation of three million—a figure, which, in the continued absence of international copyright, did not translate into massive profit for Dickens.

The inclusion of a serialized story also restricted space, so that the number of articles in each issue dropped from the eight to 10 in *Household Words* to five to seven in *All the Year Round*. This inevitably limited the variety of content, which had distinguished *Household Words*, even before Dickens placed greater emphasis on articles about foreign affairs, especially the struggle for freedom in Italy. And although Dickens published both *A Tale of Two Cities* and *Great Expectations* in the periodical, as well as *The Uncommercial Traveller* papers, he contributed proportionately less to *All the Year Round* than he had to *Household Words*. He was also far less involved in the paper's day-to-day running, especially when he was out of the country for half a year in 1867–68, during his reading tour in North America.

Third, Dickens faced greater competition in the 1860s than he had in the 1850s. Deprived of *Household Words*, Bradbury and Evans founded *Once A Week*, lavishly illustrated by major artists and serializing novels such as Charles Reade's *A Good Fight* (later retitled *The Cloister and the Hearth*). The publishers Smith, Elder achieved even greater success with their monthly magazine featuring serialized fiction, the *Cornhill Magazine*. Thackeray was its first editor, and the *Cornhill* published work by Charles Reade, Wilkie Collins, Elizabeth Gaskell, Thomas Hardy and George Eliot. Dickens tried unsuccessfully to recruit Eliot to his own periodical, but she was able to command a far higher rate from the *Cornhill* than he was prepared to offer.

Dickens's magazine suffered a further setback in 1868 when his sub-editor, W. H. Wills was seriously injured when thrown from a horse and had to retire. Having dealt with the business side of Dickens's periodicals for many years, as well as serving as a trusted confidante in Dickens's relationship with Ellen Ternan, Wills was a colleague on whom Dickens depended greatly. Quite overwhelmed by the loss, Dickens hired his son Charley as second in command, and upon Dickens's death in 1870, Charley took over the running of the periodical.

7. Dickens as Social Activist

I n the politically turbulent days of his youth and early adulthood, Dickens was an outspoken radical, or "destructive," as opponents of the Reform Act referred to liberal activists. His journalism and fiction contained vigorous social satire. He wrote for politically progressive papers and published polemical statements on specific issues; he was also personally engaged in practical social activities. Today his views are best known for his presentation of these topics in his novels, but his activism was far more committed and wide-ranging than that.

The newspapers and magazines in which he placed his work were (with the exception of the Tory *Carlton Chronicle*, to which he contributed two sketches in 1836) aligned with Reform politics. The *Monthly Magazine*, home of his earliest sketches (from 1833 to 1835), had been founded in 1796, and in its day had published radical writers including Mary Wollstonecraft and Thomas Paine. When Dickens contributed his pieces to the *Monthly*, it was owned and edited by J.B. "Captain" Holland, "as a popular mouthpiece for his ardent liberalism." A progressive newspaper, the *Morning Chronicle*, with a circulation surpassed only by *The Times*, was owned by the Liberal MP John Easthope and edited by the Benthamite John Black, along liberal principles. The weekly *Examiner*, to which Dickens frequently contributed during the 1840s and which favorably reviewed his work, had been founded as a politically radical paper by Leigh Hunt and his brother in 1808. In 1833, its literary and dramatic critic was Dickens's closest friend and adviser John Forster, who became the magazine's editor in 1847. The liberal *Daily News*, of which Dickens was the founding editor, began publication in 1846. And his own journals, *Household Words* and *All the Year Round*, voiced his progressive views as well.

Dickens's unsigned political reports for the *Morning Chronicle* were vigorously partisan, describing, for example, the behavior of

Tory supporters at the Northamptonshire hustings in 1835 as "an outrage of the most disgraceful nature I ever witnessed . . . ruffian barbarity . . . cowardly and unmanly proceeding." His pseudonymous pamphlet of 1836, *Sunday Under Three Heads*, attacked the proposed Sabbatarian legislation (which would ban recreational activities on Sundays); it was sarcastically dedicated to Charles Blomfield, Bishop of London, in recognition of his lack of "the faintest conception" of the "harmless pastimes," "innocent recreations," and "the wants and necessities" of the common people. In 1846, Dickens wrote a letter, published in the *Daily News*, in support of Ragged Schools (charity institutions that provided free education to the poor), and in 1848, two more letters penned by him on education for the poor appeared in the *Examiner*. He wrote five letters in 1846 for the *Daily News* on capital punishment, advocating the "total abolition of the Punishment of Death," and two more on the same subject, which appeared in 1849 in *The Times*.

Dickens also contributed a great many politically motivated articles on a wide range of subjects to his own journals. Many of them were not merely informative and amusing, but called out urgently for active engagement. Investigating the strike and lockout in Preston, for example, Dickens prompted both sides to submit their dispute to arbitration ("On Strike," *Household Words*, February 11, 1854). Writing about Ragged Schools, he urged that an annual sum "contemptible in amount . . . would relieve the prisons, diminish preposterous Red Tape conditions, clear loads of shame and guilt out of the streets . . ." etc. ("A Sleep to Startle Us," *Household Words* March 13, 1852). Observing that governmental inertia is ubiquitously blamed on "Nobody," he called upon "Somebody" to relieve "the great fire raging in the land" ("Nobody, Somebody and Everybody," *Household Words* August 30, 1856).

Much admired and sought after as a public speaker, Dickens delivered the great majority of his speeches in support of self-help organizations and charities. Benevolent institutions, mechanics' institutes, hospitals, sanatoriums, and funds in support of writers, artists, and professional theatrical people, all received rousing commendation and encouragement from him. Moreover, the amateur dramatic productions which he organized and starred in were frequently in support of a good cause: *Not So Bad As We Seem* was presented in 1851 to raise money for the Guild of Literature and Art; *The Frozen Deep* was revived in 1857 for benefit performances in aid of the family of the recently deceased dramatist Douglas Jerrold. Dickens's motives were not always entirely altruistic, however; he was always strongly motivated by his enjoyment of these activities.

His novels are filled with trenchant satire on social issues: the Poor Law in *Oliver Twist*, the Yorkshire Schools in *Nicholas Nickleby*, the obfuscations of Chancery in *Bleak House*, utilitarian narrow-mindedness in *Hard Times*, and the red tape of burcaucracy in *Little Dorrit*. In each of these works, Dickens cut through the arguments for a particular issue and the complexities that made constructive action difficult. His goal in doing so was to identify, clarify, and simplify these subjects to lay bare the pith of the matter and to ask, in the name of humanity, if a remedy could be made possible.

And Dickens involved himself in social activism in more ways than in writing. In 1838, for example, he spent many nights backstage with his good friend the tragedian William Charles Macready, discussing and advising on Macready's aspiration of restoring English drama to its former glory. The centerpiece was the actor's monumental production of *King Lear* at Covent Garden, which rejected the 153-year tradition of staging the play in Colley Cibber's revised version, returning instead to Shakespeare's original text. The consultations led not only to the most important Shakespearean production of the 19th century, but also fed into Dickens's own writing, visibly influencing *The Old Curiosity Shop*, *Dombey and Son*, and other works.

At a time of cholera epidemics, stench from the open sewer that was the Thames, streets awash with horse manure, appalling slums, ignorance, and crime, Dickens was active in a number of reform organizations. In 1849, he addressed the Newsvendors' Benevolent Association and later became its president, following James Harmer, the radical lawyer famous for opposing miscarriages of justice, on whom the character of Jaggers in *Great Expectations* was based. Along with novelist and playwright Bulwer Lytton, Dickens founded and worked hard (although ultimately unsuccessfully) in support of the Guild of Literature and Art, a benevolent association for writers and artists. He also collaborated on various projects with key 19th-century social activists such as Thomas Southwood Smith, James Kay-Shuttleworth, Lord Ashley (later Lord Shaftesbury), and his brother-in-law Henry Austin. Convinced that sanitary improvements took priority over all other causes, and outspoken about drunkenness being the result of poverty rather than its cause, Dickens campaigned for effective central, government-backed authority to coordinate action and confront opposition. During the Crimean War (1853–1856), he was a member of his friend Sir Austen Henry Layard's Administrative Reform Association, aimed at reducing red tape.

Less grandly, Dickens served as unofficial patron to aspiring writers, little known in their day and long forgotten by posterity, offering help and advice to the likes of William Thom (1799-1848), the weaver poet from Inverurie; Thomas John Ousley (1805-1874), author of *Death's Destruction*, a sub-Miltonic epic; and John Overs (1808-1844), whose proofs of *Evenings of a Working Man* Dickens corrected in 1844.

By far his most important social activism, however, emerged from Dickens's association with the wealthy heiress and philanthropist Angela Burdett-Coutts, for whom he worked tirelessly as adviser, manager, and almoner. Their first project together came in 1843, when Dickens sent Miss Coutts a "sledge-hammer account" of his visit to inspect the Field Lane Ragged School in Holborn. There, he watched volunteer teachers valiantly confront "prodigious misery and ignorance" in a rotten building, "precisely such a place as Fagin lived in," and where "the seeds of certain ruin are sown." His recommendations were above all practical: he urged that bathing facilities were a priority, before any possibility of learning could occur and, although deferential to Miss Coutts's strong religious convictions, he deplored the bickering between different faiths as the foremost obstacle to improvement. Although Dickens's attempts to attract government support were unsuccessful at the time, Miss Coutts sent a donation, and the Ragged School Union flourished; eventually, the 1870 Education Act created a comprehensive system of elementary education, superseding the Ragged Schools.

Dickens also assisted Miss Coutts in a project of slum clearance and housing development. He took her to inspect model houses built by the Society for Improving the Condition of the Labouring Classes in Bloomsbury and helped her in planning the housing scheme in Nova Scotia Gardens, Bethnal Green, in East London. This site of poverty, stench and disease, lacking drainage and littered with vile houses made of rotting timber, was notorious for crime and was a known haunt of body snatchers. On Dickens's recommendation, Miss Coutts had five-story tenements built for working class families, equipped with reading rooms and washing facilities. These structures were designed around a courtyard "instead of the absurd and expensive separate walnut shells" in which residents had been previously crowded.

Their most significant collaboration, however, was the founding of Urania Cottage for homeless women in Shepherd's Bush. In a particularly long and detailed letter of May 26, 1846, Dickens spelled out to Miss Coutts his ideas for the home. Its name (which belonged to the house before it was purchased) was an epithet for Aphrodite, meaning "celestial," and reflected the idea of a place of gentle encouragement to reformation, rather than a harsh, punitive institution. He urged practical instruction before religious training; punctuality, cleanliness, domestic duties, and encouragement through a grading system to prepare the residents for emigration and the possibility of marriage after they left the Home. Dickens rejected advice that the women should be given sober clothing, arguing instead for neat and modest, but colorful, garments. Although intended in the first instance to rehabilitate prostitutes, Urania was also a refuge for all helpless and hopeless women. Their past histories were kept confidential, and they were forbidden to maintain contact with former associates, to ensure that they would not relapse.

Dickens threw himself into the planning and day-to-day operation of Urania. He interviewed and hired the staff and residents; he chaired monthly governance meetings, visited often, and made himself available to deal at a moment's notice when difficulties arose. His initial recommendation was for a cohort of about 30 women, but the final number was less than 15. He hoped for a success rate of around 50 percent, and eventually the result was slightly higher than that.

Tantalizingly, Dickens kept a copious "case-book," as he called it, noting down details of his many long interviews with the women—almost certainly a sourcebook for elements in his subsequent fiction. However, it was lost, no doubt irrevocably.

Dickens dedicated *Martin Chuzzlewit* to Miss Coutts; she, in turn, acted as godmother to his eldest son Charley and subsidized his schooling at Eton. For years, he sent her advance proofs of his writings and was in close personal contact with her, but their association came to an abrupt end after his separation from his wife. Miss Coutts tried to reunite them but, having failed, she broke off all contact with Dickens. She also stopped funding Urania Cottage, which closed for good in 1862.

Dickens was far from indiscriminate in his charitable activities; from the outset of his career, he composed stinging satire on misguided philanthropy. From the Reverend Mr. Stiggins in *Pickwick* to the blustering Mr. Honeythunder in *Edwin Drood*, Dickens railed against what he saw as cant, notably that of doctrinaire enthusiasts, such as the aggressive condescension of Mrs. Pardiggle in *Bleak House*. His suspicion of Evangelical enthusiasm made his long and fruitful association with Miss Coutts, who was devoutly religious, all the more remarkable. He also supported the emigration schemes of humanitarian activist Caroline Chisholm, model for the "telescopic philanthropy" of *Bleak Houses*'s Mrs. Jellyby, in her campaign to convert the natives of Borrioboola-Gha, on the left bank of the Niger.

One form of public service that did *not* interest Dickens was becoming a member of Parliament. On at least four occasions between 1841 and 1868, he turned down invitations to stand for election, having acquired a hearty contempt for politicians during his days as a parliamentary reporter. As he said a few months before he died, "My faith in the people governing is, on the whole infinitesimal; my faith in the people governed is, on the whole, illimitable."

8. At the height of his powers

Having undertaken a searching revaluation of his life and art, Dickens proceeded to write what is widely considered as his masterpiece. In its huge array of inter-related characters, variety of moods and tones, inventive dual narrative, thrilling mystery plot, and searching social analysis, Bleak House is grand in scale and magnificent in achievement. An eminent scholar has even compared this novel to the Sistine Chapel as one of the great works of Western art. But while Michelangelo depicted stories from the Book of Genesis in celebration of Renaissance humanism, the vision of Bleak House was radically different, as Dickens evoked a return to prehistoric chaos—a depiction of active "uncreation"—to excoriate Victorian England. In the opening paragraphs, the absence of finite verbs brilliantly conveyed a sense of random, purposeless activity, "as if the waters had but newly retired from the face of the earth, and it would not be wonderful to meet a Megalosaurus, forty feet long or so, waddling like an elephantine lizard up Holborn Hill." The setting is enveloped in fog, real and metaphoric, and the Court of Chancery, "most pestilent of hoary sinners," reaches its tentacles everywhere. Despair, desolation, and death dominate the scene, and yet buoyant hope, sparkling style, and exhilarating comedy leaven the gloom. It is an extraordinary book.

While it was gestating in Dickens's mind, the mood of the nation was, by contrast, that of triumphalism. From May to October of 1851, the Great Exhibition, a world fair promoted by Prince Albert, "displayed all that is useful or beautiful in art." The event was organized to showcase the country's industrial leadership, social stability, power, and security, as well as economic strength. Symbolic of national superiority, half of the exhibits were British. Reporting on the opening ceremony at the Crystal Palace on the first of May, The Times commented:

> Some saw in it the second and more glorious inauguration

of their SOVEREIGN; some a solemn dedication of art and its store; some were most reminded of that day when all ages and climes shall be gathered round the throne of their MAKER.

It was estimated that six million people in England and Wales—approximately a third of the entire population—visited the exhibition, and it generated a huge income, which was used afterward to build the Victoria and Albert Museum, the Natural History Museum, and the Science Museum. Dickens, however, was not impressed. Its promoters hoped, as he noted in "The Last Words of the Old Year"—the lead article in the first issue of *Household Words* in 1851—that that Great Exhibition would witness "a great assemblage of the peaceful glories of the world." But, Dickens believed the exhibition glossed over the problems of the Victorian era and misrepresented the reality. He wrote:

> Which of my children shall behold the Princes, Prelates, Nobles, Merchants, of England, equally united, for another Exhibition—for a great display of England's sins and negligences, to be, by steady contemplation of all eyes, and steady union of all hearts and hands, set right? Come hither
> . . .

Bleak House began serial publication three months after the Great Exhibition closed. The book was Dickens's riposte to England's complacency and self-congratulation during that event. He centered his attack on the Court of Chancery, which he boldly deployed as an organizing principle throughout the book. While other novels, including his own, had developed thematic unity with some sophistication (Jane Austen's works spring immediately to mind), this was the first time an institution had figured as a novel's symbolic center, and many subsequent authors have followed that path—Franz Kafka, Arthur Koestler, Bernard Malamud, Aleksandr Solzhenitsyn, and William Styron, to name just a few.

The Court of Chancery was a legal body of great antiquity.

Founded as a court of equity, its mandate was to protect the rights of otherwise defenseless people, such as lunatics and infants. It had a wider remit than common law courts, and from Elizabethan times was notorious for high costs, backlogs, and delays. Unsuccessful attempts had been made over the centuries to deal with its abuses. In 1851, the government proposed in the Queen's speech to deal with its inefficiency. The Times began a running attack; while Dickens was writing, and in following years, important procedural reforms improved matters.

Dickens had previously written about Chancery abuses in Pickwick, and in 1844, he was himself embroiled in a series of Chancery suits, when he took some "vagabonds" to court for piracy of A Christmas Carol, in flagrant breach of copyright. He won his case but was left with court costs of over £700. "I shall not easily forget the expense, and anxiety, and horrible injustice," he wrote later. In Bleak House, Chancery provides employment (and amusement) for the lawyers; it drives poor Miss Flite insane, maddens Gridley, the man from Shropshire, and it breaks the heart of Richard Carstone. It also sets the main plot in motion, when Lady Dedlock, observed by Tulkinghorn, faints on seeing handwriting on a court document, copied by her former lover.

The obfuscation of Chancery proceedings is symbolized by the fog in the book's opening paragraphs. It is also the foremost example of the theme of irresponsibility, especially evident in the paradigm of dysfunctional families, which pervades the entire novel. When the Lord Chancellor meets Richard and Ada, wards of Chancery, in his chambers, Esther observes that "at his best [he] appeared so poor a substitute for the love and pride of parents." In the next chapter we meet the model of "telescopic philanthropy," a term Dickens coined to describe Mrs. Jellyby, who is obsessed with saving the natives in faraway Nigeria while neglecting her own family. The book is peopled with orphans—Richard, Ada, Esther, Jo, Guster, and Charley—with bad parents, including Skimpole, Pardiggle and Turveydrop; and with inverted families such as the Bagnets and the Smallweeds. Irresponsibility also figures in the satire on government by Boodle, Coodle and Doodle, in the ruinous slum of Tom-All-Alone's, "avoided by all decent people," and in the jurisdiction of Chancery, "of course."

In the book, irresponsibility is predicated on inability or unwillingness to see through the fog and recognize the relations which each character shares with others. One of the extraordinary features of *Bleak House* is the sheer extent of hidden interconnectedness. The book is full of detectives—not simply Inspector Bucket, the first great detective in English fiction, but also the amateur sleuths trying to ferret out secrets: Tulkinghorn, Guppy, Krook, Smallweed, and Mrs. Snagsby. As the plots unfold, we learn that Sir Leicester's housekeeper is the mother of Trooper George, Mrs. Smallweed is the sister of Krook, and Mrs. Chadband was once a servant to Esther's godmother. In this context, it is hardly a surprise when we discover that the fiery maid Hortense has been a patron at George's Shooting Gallery. The foremost secret, of course, which drives the novel's accelerating momentum, is Lady Dedlock's hidden past, which ties everything together in the end.

On the other hand, Esther Summerson, the story's first-person narrator, is a true Christian heroine. Conceived in original sin and told it would have been better if she had not been born, Esther responds—not with sullen paranoia like Miss Wade in *Little Dorrit*, but with selfless and unobtrusive determination to offer practical, personal help to everyone with whom she comes into contact. The clear moral evoked by the Jellyby household is that charity begins at home; in the novel as a whole, Dickens insists upon the need to recognize and act on one's responsibility to others.

In this novel, personal relationships and social responsibilities are important themes. Dickens targeted his satire against the monstrous legal system at the book's core, as well as at governmental ineptitude, slum conditions, class and religious prejudice, and other key issues of his day. The book is grounded on pressing, real conditions in Victorian England, but interwoven, in quintessentially Dickensian manner, with what he called dwelling on "the romantic side of familiar things." *Bleak House* ends in a true fairy-tale fashion as the heroine's secret wish is granted as if by magic, so that she can live happily ever after.

This combination of realism and fancy sparked public controversy between Dickens and George Eliot's consort, George Henry Lewes. He argued that the spontaneous combustion by which Krook died was a scientific impossibility. Dickens defended himself by noting that "These are mysteries we can't account for!" And in his private correspondence to Lewes, he cited several cases of spontaneous combustion, including that of an Italian countess, Cornelia di Bandi, who had reportedly died that way in 1731. Disputes aside, Dickens's readers have always felt that whatever its physical impossibility, the death of the low-life "Lord Chancellor" is one of the great symbolic triumphs of the book. Dickens wrote the novel in a daring dual narrative, dividing the story-telling between a witty, satirical, and omniscient present-tense voice which stood aloof outside the novel, and that of Esther, the quiet, compassionate and shrewd young woman who retrospectively shows us how to live in an imperfect world. In a letter to the daughter of Lord Denman penned in December 1852, Dickens underlined his seriousness of purpose:

> Pray do not suppose that I ever write merely to amuse or without an object. I wish I were as clear of every offense before Heaven, as I am of that. I may try to insinuate it into people's hearts sometimes, in preference to knocking them down and breaking their heads with it . . . but I always have it. Without it, my pursuit—and the steadiness, patience, seclusion, regularity, hard work and self-concentration, it demands—would be utterly worthless to me.

Dickens's usual artist, Hablot Browne ("Phiz") illustrated *Bleak House* in what is generally thought to be their most successful collaboration. The "dark plate" technique he used created an overall cast evoking the somber tone of the book. When Dickens completed *Bleak House* in December 1853, he planned to stop writing for a year, but a serious dip in sales of *Household Words* made him determined to confront the problem by introducing a new serial story into the pages of his periodical. This involved a return to weekly deadlines for the first time since *Barnaby Rudge* in 1841, and he found it difficult to fit content into the "teaspoon" size of the installments. Published between April 1 and August 12, 1854, *Hard Times* is the shortest of his novels, and the only one set entirely out of London. It had mixed critical reception, but its brevity, and the endorsement of the influential critic F. R. Leavis in 1948, have made it a frequent choice for school and university courses.

Hard Times is not only the shortest of Dickens's novels, but it is also his most abstract and polemical. The brevity and sharp focus ensure that the satire on the philosophy of fact and the defense of fancy are presented with great forcefulness and clarity, but they also reduce the complexity of his art, as comparison of Sleary's circus troupe with Vincent Crummles's theatrical company reveals. Sleary, conceived to embody the value of providing entertainment and to evince the outlook underlying his profession, lacks the comic ebullience of Crummles. Kidderminster and Childers are not afforded the room to develop which gives Folair and Snevellicci such engaging expansiveness, and Sissy Jupe, not a performer at all, is detached from the circus in the book's opening scenes. It is also odd that this book about the importance of "fancy" over "fact" should be Dickens's least expansive and colorful novel.

Moreover, Dickens entirely sidestepped the fact that, as he well knew, the circus was one of the foremost examples of the evolution of entertainment in the 19th century. It is a telling touch of irony that the entertainers appear to be far more dedicated and hard-working than Bounderby or even Gradgrind, but it is not apparent that they are also engaged in an increasingly commercialized activity. Dickens himself, fully committed to financial exploitation of his talents, could easily have shown this side of the circus enterprise, but instead, he chose to simplify and sentimentalize his entertainers.

Before embarking on this novel, just as he had taken a fact-finding trip to Yorkshire in preparation for writing *Nicholas Nickleby*, Dickens paid a lightning visit to Preston, in the north of England, where a strike and lockout had shut down the local mills for many weeks. "On Strike," his essay in *Household Words* reporting on what he saw and heard, revealed that he was aware that union leaders were not all blustering demagogues like Slackbridge in the novel—but then, he also knew that all industrialists were not buffoons like Bounderby. In the novel, the two characters offset each other to make Dickens's point that mutual respect and understanding between owners and workers were a precondition for sound industrial relations. But by having his representative hand, Stephen Blackpool, stand aside from his workmates during the strike and by deleting a passage in manuscript, which explained Stephen's motive, Dickens weakened his case.

The issues raised in the novel are wide-ranging. The opening scene in a schoolroom confronts contemporary worries that measures then being implemented to expand the provision of education in England were replacing genuine acquisition of knowledge with rote learning—a memorization technique based on repetition.

The Bitzer character is Dickens's contribution to that debate. Gradgrind's philosophy of fact satirizes the rationalist views of Jeremy Bentham and Adam Smith, which Dickens considered misguided in their dismissal of imagination and feeling as the source of moral value. The plight of Stephen echoes Dickens's growing dissatisfaction with his own marriage, and even as the novel was being serialized in *Household Words* the periodical carried articles on the near-impossibility of obtaining divorce.

The book's principal achievement is the tragic history at its heart. Thomas Gradgrind, well-intentioned but misguided, blights the lives of his children with his doctrinaire theories and, as events unfold, is forced into an agonizing revaluation. His daughter Louisa, helplessly yearning to fill the emotional emptiness left by her upbringing, is easy prey to a selfish brother, a boastfully obtuse husband, and an idle seducer, but has just enough imaginative sensibility—that quality which Dickens believed "innate in the human breast"—to save herself from utter ruin. With consummate delicacy, Dickens unveils the issues and their results in the two parallel scenes between father and daughter. In the first, Louisa gazes forlornly out the window at the "languid and monotonous" factory smoke, observing that "when the night comes, Fire bursts out!"–an outcome that follows inexorably, with her repressed emotions eventually erupting as she is tempted by a would-be seducer; she flees and collapses at her father's feet.

Before he turned to his succeeding novel in 1855, Dickens faced grave concerns both publicly and privately. The mismanagement of the Crimean War–as he said in a speech, it was unbearable to him that the *Comedy of Errors* played like a tragedy–led him to become more politically active than at any other time in his career, joining Austen Layard's Administrative Reform Association. His unhappiness with his marriage left him restless and discontented, and an unexpected reunion with former flame Maria Beadnell, now 40 years old and fat, was profoundly disillusioning. In that frame of mind, Dickens proceeded to write the most somber of his books, *Little Dorrit*, in which all the characters are confined to prison of one sort or another, and the hero is a middle-aged man, lonely, hopeless and unfulfilled. Maria is caricatured as Flora Finching, silly and garrulous. And while memories of his father had previously inspired the ebullient comic figure of Wilkins Micawber, the same original led to the brooding portrait of William Dorrit, irretrievably damaged by imprisonment for debt.

Uncharacteristically, Dickens had great difficulty in getting started with the novel and considered throwing it over and starting again. Always needing a suitable title before he could proceed, he jettisoned his initial choice, "Nobody's Fault," after writing several chapters, calling it *Little Dorrit* instead. The revised focus on his heroine, signaling a more optimistic vision of his materials, enabled him to move forward.

More tightly claustrophobic than any other of his works, *Little Dorrit* opens in a prison cell in Marseilles, moves to a ship in quarantine in the harbor, then to the home of Mrs. Clennam, confined to a wheelchair, and on to the Marshalsea debtors' prison, where the heroine was born and where she lives with the feckless family she struggles to support. The entire country is obstructed by the red tape of the Circumlocution Office, and social snobbery restricts free relationships. Soon nearly everyone—Mrs. Merdle's parrot in its cage, the paranoid Miss Wade, the workhouse inmate Nandy, and the swindling financier Merdle (constantly seen clasping his wrists "in a constabulary manner" as he hides behind doors from his butler)—is shown to be in a state of imprisonment. The book is structured ironically in two halves, with the Dorrit family initially confined within the walls of the Marshalsea, only to suffer far greater psychological imprisonment after their release. In an extraordinary scene near the book's end, Mr. Dorrit collapses at a formal dinner party in Rome and imagines himself back at the debtors' prison.

Arthur Clennam, the saddest hero Dickens ever created, finds emptiness and frustration wherever he turns, until he is ultimately rescued by the heroine's love. One influential critic described Little Dorrit herself, Amy, as a "paraclete," or Holy Spirit, who redeems the fallen world. Echoing the expulsion of Adam and Eve from Eden at the end of *Paradise Lost*, Amy and Arthur walk from their wedding, "inseparable and blessed; and as they passed along in sunshine and in shade, the noisy and eager, and the arrogant and the froward and the vain, fretted and chafed, and made their usual uproar." It is by far the most downbeat ending to any of Dickens's works; the utter implausibility of the will affecting their ultimate happiness confirms the unlikelihood that anyone, however virtuous, can escape the all-pervasive prisons Dickens has imagined.

9. New love

Momentous personal events had intervened before Dickens embarked on his next novel. In 1856, while he was in the middle of writing *Little Dorrit*, Gad's Hill Place, the home he idealized since childhood, came on the market. He bought it, moving permanently out of London a few years later. That autumn he worked closely with Wilkie Collins to prepare a production of Collins's play *The Frozen Deep*. The play dramatized the bitter rivalry between two men for the woman they both loved and the self-sacrifice of one character (played by Dickens) to save the life of his rival. Initially, the cast consisted of friends and family members, but when the production moved in the summer to Manchester for public performances, amateur actresses were replaced by professionals, leading to Dickens's fateful meeting with Ellen Ternan. When the play finished, Dickens and Collins left on a supposedly random expedition, which they wrote up for *All the Year Round* as *The Lazy Tour of Two Idle Apprentices*. However, from the outset, Dickens planned to end up in Doncaster, where Ellen was appearing at the local theater during race week. By the following spring, Dickens was deeply in love, had separated from Catherine and commenced the first of his public reading programs, starting in London and then touring the provinces, Ireland, and Scotland.

Intimations of mortality and growing unhappiness in his marriage fed into this crisis over several years. In 1848, Dickens's beloved older sister Fanny had died, followed shortly after by her crippled son Henry, on whom the Tiny Tim character was based. In 1851, his father, whom he came to love and admire after the earlier worries and exasperations, died following "the most terrible operation known in surgery," on a diseased bladder, without anaesthesia—a procedure, which left the room "a slaughter house of blood." Two weeks later, his frail infant daughter Dora Annie died, while Catherine was undergoing treatment for a depressive illness.

Restless and unsettled, Dickens lamented to Forster: "Why is it, that as with poor David [Copperfield], a sense comes crushing on me now, when I fall into low spirits, as of one happiness I have missed in life, and one friend and companion I have never made?" Again to Forster, he confided that "the skeleton in my domestic closet is becoming a pretty big one." And then, "Poor Catherine and I are not made for each other, and there is no help for it." In October 1857, he had the door between his dressing room and the marital bedroom sealed, and in May 1858, he called in lawyers to effect a formal separation. He and Catherine had been married for 22 years, had 10 children, and she had suffered several miscarriages. Dickens was to claim that the marriage had been unhappy from the start, but surviving letters show that this retrospective judgment was untrue, and it is hard for even the most fervent admirers to applaud Dickens's behavior at this time.

Ignoring advice from friends and lawyers, Dickens made a public statement, which he titled "Personal," about the marital break-up, publishing it first in *The Times* and then in *Household Words*. It was reprinted widely, both in Britain and North America, and promptly aroused adverse publicity. Matters were made even worse when a letter, which Dickens had written to his readings manager—the so-called "violated letter"—was published in the *New York Tribune* on August 16 and widely reprinted. In it, he claimed that Catherine suffered from "a mental disorder." Dickens's explanation of "incompatibility" (a word that, in fact, did not appear in either of his statements) elicited a loud chorus of dismay, outrage, and satire.

The fallout from the collapse of his marriage included the end of several friendships, notably with Mark Lemon, editor of *Punch* who advised on Catherine's behalf during the separation; it also sparked a quarrel with his publishers Bradbury and Evans when they refused to print Dickens's personal statement regarding the separation in *Punch*, another of their publications. Furious, Dickens closed down *Household Words* and inaugurated *All the Year Round* in its place, taking over as the publisher and editor of his new journal. He did not attend his son Charley's wedding to the daughter of Frederick Evans, and he never spoke to Catherine again.

At the time of the separation, rumors were rife. Ellen was actually named in the American press, although not, so far as is known, in Britain. Thackeray was alleged to have spread gossip about Dickens and "an actress," leading to unpleasantness at the Garrick Club, from which Dickens's protégé Edmund Yates was expelled. Clearly, Dickens's family and closest friends knew about Ellen, but it took more than half a century for the liaison to become widely known. Given the extent of Dickens's fame and the volume of information we have about other aspects of his life, it is astonishing–and tantalizing–how little is known for certain. Was Ellen his mistress? The likelihood is great, but there is no hard proof. Did they have a child who died? Again, there is circumstantial evidence but no proof. Did Dickens suffer his final stroke not at Gad's Hill, as was announced at the time, but in her house, as a recent biographer has speculated? Did Ellen attend his private interment in Westminster Abbey? There was much speculation, but Dickens covered his tracks well, and these parts of his life remain elusive.

A few facts, however, are certain. For instance, Dickens first met Ellen when she played a minor role in the Manchester production of *The Frozen Deep*. There is a passage in *The Lazy Tour*, in which the Dickens character is wildly infatuated:

> Mr Goodchild [the Dickens character] . . . is suspected . . . to have fallen into a dreadful state concerning a pair of little lilac gloves and a little bonnet that he saw there [at the race meeting at Doncaster, where the Ternans were performing]. Mr Idle [the character based on Wilkie Collins] asserts, that he did afterwards repeat at the Angel, with an appearance of being lunatically seized, some rhapsody to the following effect: "O little lilac gloves! And O winning little bonnet, making in conjunction with her golden hair quite a Glory in the sunlight round the pretty head, why anything in the world but you and me!"

There was also a letter from Dickens to J. B. Buckstone, manager of the Haymarket Theatre, seeking an engagement for Ellen. Then there are records of houses, in which Ellen lived in London, paid for by a "Mr. Tringham." Ellen and her mother were in a compartment in a railway carriage with Dickens at the time of the Staplehurst accident in 1865. Dickens looked into the possibility of Ellen joining him during his reading tour of North America in 1867–68. There are references in his letters to the "riddle" and to the "patient," which almost certainly refer to Ellen. And Dickens was frequently in France for unspecified purposes in the last decade of his life. Ellen was named as a beneficiary in his will.

And that was all, save a novel in 1929 and a newspaper article in 1934. But in 1935–65 years after Dickens's death and 21 after Ellen's passing–a biography by Thomas Wright claimed that Ellen had been Dickens's mistress, basing his case on the authority of a clergyman who purported to have been told of the relationship by Ellen herself. Wright proposed that Ellen inspired the characters of the cold Estella in *Great Expectations* and the petulant Bella Wilfer in *Our Mutual Friend*. The Dickens establishment vigorously denied Wright's disclosures, but scholars since that time have unearthed supporting evidence, most recently relating Dickens's known movements in 1862–63 with the timing of human gestation, which seems to confirm that there was indeed a child who died. The evidence is not conclusive, but it is persuasive.

All this matters not as gossip, but because this information led to a radical revaluation of Dickens's achievement as a novelist. In 1939, the American critic Edmund Wilson published an essay, "Dickens: the Two Scrooges," which, as the title suggests, presented a writer deeply divided against himself, outwardly jovial and contented but inwardly tortured and pessimistic. Just over a decade later, a major new biography by Edgar Johnson entitled *Charles Dickens: His Tragedy and Triumph*, portrayed Dickens as a radically complex writer and not simply the cheerful man who celebrated Christmas at Dingley Dell, wrote moving deathbed scenes, and created great comic characters. Rather, it presented him as a person whose writing also plumbed dark psychological depths of the human condition and offered searching analysis of not just social issues but of civilization itself. Dickens's reputation grew exponentially, from being seen as a cheerful storyteller suitable mainly for children, to a colossus of Western literature.

Referring to Dickens, George Orwell noted that "sexual love is almost entirely outside his scope" and dismissed his heroines as "legless angels." There are several ways to respond to this charge. First, just as late 19th and early 20th century writers reacted against what they saw as Victorian prudery, so, decades earlier, Victorian writers spoke out against what they considered as the prurience and vulgarity of the more libertine Regency, and catered to a wider audience by cleaning up their books. Second, one can accept that sexual love was not a primary subject for Dickens, although his depictions of the frustrations of Rosa Dartle and Bradley Headstone, to go no further, show that there were aspects of sexual love he was fully prepared to confront. And when he moved away from the heroines whom he invariably idealized and spiritualized, he was perfectly capable of depicting a sexually mature female character, such as Miss Snevellicci, and there is no telling what he might have done with Helena Landless had he lived to develop her character more fully. Moreover, he created many female characters of varied range: daughters, sisters, estranged wives, elderly women, and (best of all) comic grotesque figures like Mrs. Gamp.

Like many people in his and other eras, Dickens had varied and complex relationships with the opposite sex. He caricatured his mother as the inanely garrulous Mrs. Nickleby, but she seems to have been an important influence on his comic outlook and his sense of fun. His childhood love for Lucy Stroughill was an innocent romance; his frustrated feelings for Maria Beadnell were crucially formative, and later turned upside down when she reappeared in his life—as silly and flirtatious as ever but no longer young and charming. For years, he valued Catherine as a companion, sexual partner, and domestic anchor, although that latter role at some point was usurped by Catherine's younger sister Georgina, who stayed on as his loyal, adoring housekeeper after the marriage collapsed. The fact that Mary Hogarth died at 17 meant that he could safely idealize her as an unattainable icon. His daughter Katey left him in tears when she married Charles Collins to get, he thought, away from home. The evidence suggests that she was the most vibrant of all his children. His other daughter Mamie idolized him and never married. And we simply do not know to what extent Ellen Ternan satisfied his needs and aspirations; what we can be sure of is that he loved her intensely from the summer when they first met to the day he died more than a dozen years later.

10. Splendid strolling: The public readings

O f all the values Dickens espoused, the most cherished was surely conviviality. The image of friends and family gathered together, cheerful and relaxed in each other's company, happily sharing stories, food, drink, and conversation was his foremost conception of social harmony, as represented by the Cratchit family sitting by the fireside after Christmas dinner. In his stories, his narrative persona, welcoming and congenial, invites readers into personal communion with him, and his depictions of entertainment stressed the relationship between performer and audience. Often he devoted as much attention in his writings to the auditors and spectators as to the actors. Master Humphrey's cronies sitting at his clock-side; Kit and Barbara taking their families to Astley's; the working class patrons in "Two Views of a Cheap Theatre;" the "Round of Stories by the Christmas Fire" in the 1852 and 1853 Christmas issues of *Household Words*, and seven poor travelers in the Christmas edition for 1854: these are but a few instances. It is entirely appropriate, therefore, that he chose, at the height of his powers, to develop a new form of convivial entertainment, which would strengthen his bonds with his readers.

"It was characteristic of Dickens," observed Philip Collins, editor of the public reading texts, that he sought refuge at a time of personal misery "not in reclusion or misanthropy but . . . in seeing and amusing his public." The decision to embark on readings from his works marked a major shift in focus, away from writing and editing—although he was not giving up those activities—and towards a renewed commitment to public performance. There were three determining factors behind the move. First, conscious of a large number of dependents, he was able to make a great deal more money quicker and with less continuous effort than by writing long works of prose fiction. Second, it brought increased intimacy with his admirers. Introducing his first reading for profit, he remarked, "whatever brings a public man and his public face to face, on terms of mutual confidence and respect, is a good thing"–a point underlined by the distinguished Victorian scholar Kathleen Tillotson, who shrewdly judged that "when all is said . . . his life-long love-affair with his reading public . . . is by far the most interesting love-affair of his life." Third, it provided a means of exploiting his fascination with all things theatrical, in a unique type of performance in which he was the scriptwriter, producer, director, and solo actor. His closest advisor, John Forster, considered the shows to be vulgar showmanship, declaring that "it was a substitution of lower for higher aims." The audiences, however, were enraptured: "Hear Dickens and die," wrote one reviewer, "you will never live to hear anything of its kind so good."

His active engagement with the theater extended throughout Dickens's life. One of the first volumes, which he consulted on getting a reader's ticket to the British Museum at the age of 18, was a multi-volume edition of Shakespeare edited by the suggestively named Samuel Weller Singer. He was also active in a short-lived Shakespeare Club and its successor, the Shakespeare Society, of which he was a Council member in 1843–44. In 1832, before he began writing for a living, Dickens applied for an audition as an actor, and the next year he mounted family theatrical productions at his parents' home in Bentinck Street. His early sketch, "Mrs Joseph Porter," draws on that experience. At the same time as writing his first sketches, Dickens also tried to make his name as a playwright. Having written his first play, *Misnar, Sultan of India*, at the age of nine, in 1836 he revised the tale of "The Great Winglebury Duel" as a comic burletta, which ran at the St. James's Theatre for more than 50 performances. That same year he collaborated with John Hullah on an operetta, *The Village Coquettes*, and wrote two farces, *Is She His Wife?* and *The Lamplighter*, but none of them was successful. In the 1840s, he wrote a number of theater reviews for the *Examiner*, and while in Canada in 1842, he took part in a theatrical production.

Later that year Dickens wrote a prologue for Westland Marston's play, *The Patrician's Daughter*. He produced and took the leading role in several ambitious amateur theatrical productions, two of which—Ben Jonson's *Every Man in His Humour* in 1845 and *The Frozen Deep* in 1857—included command performances before the Queen. Other productions included Fletcher and Massinger's *The Elder Brother* in 1846, Shakespeare's *Merry Wives of Windsor* in 1848, Bulwer's *Not So Bad As We Seem* in 1851, and Collins's *The Lighthouse* in 1855.

One-man or -woman performances were a frequent attraction in 19th-century Britain. Dickens's favorite actor was Charles Mathews (1776–1835), whose quick-change solo routines he went to see "whenever he played." Samuel Taylor Coleridge, Hazlitt, Carlyle, and Thackeray were among literary personages who gave lecture series; Fanny Kemble gave a popular series of recitations from Shakespeare in 1848; and for several years in the 1850s, Albert Smith's entertainment describing his ascent of Mont Blanc was the most popular attraction in London. Smith's brother Arthur was Dickens's first readings manager until forced to resign because of poor health. Most extraordinary of all, immediately after Dickens retired from his readings, a clergyman who gloried in the name of John Chippendale Montesquieu Bellew recited the text of *Hamlet* while a troupe of actors mimed the actions; their complete silence preserving the fastidious from the wickedness of attending an actual play.

But Dickens was the first author to give readings from his own works, and they proved enormously popular. Forster judged that it was from the readings, "as much as by his books, the world knew him in his later life." The readings were distinctive in a number of ways. First, unlike Mathews's quick-change routine, Dickens performed in his own dress, appearing on stage as himself, and establishing personal rapport with his audience. For the initial performances, he prefaced his act with a brief statement, but thereafter he proceeded straight to the reading as soon as he walked onto the stage. He created characters in distinctive speech tones and mannerisms, but he spoke the narrative in his own voice, thus emphasizing his role as author, speaking as a friend. Without change of costume and with no props beyond a book and a reading desk, Dickens presented himself as himself, without disguise.

Audiences marveled at his ability to bring characters to life just through voice and gestures. In stark contrast to the highly stylized delivery of contemporary acting idiom, in which actors declaimed melodramatically, Dickens's method was impersonation, in which he stepped out of his own self and assumed the personality and mannerisms of each of his characters. "He do the police in different voices," Betty Higden says in *Our Mutual Friend*, of Sloppy's reading abilities; so Dickens was perceived actually to *become* each character he presented.

Thoroughly professional, Dickens oversaw every detail of the arrangements in the halls where he performed, and, when on tour, he refused hospitality even from close friends. He prepared meticulously, rehearsing hundreds of times to bring a reading to the state of perfection, which he required. Although he held a book in his hand, in fact, he knew each routine by heart, and he regularly varied details from performance to performance, as audiences discovered when they tried to follow his performance with a volume open before them. This way, he was actively creating his characters as he spoke. There was a basic consonance between the kind of novels he composed and the kind of acting he presented. Nothing defines the nature of his artistry so clearly as the relation between his reading and his writings. Appearing on stage, he said while rehearsing *The Frozen Deep*, was like "writing a book in company."

Just as Dickens took pride in the accomplishment of his novels, so too he gained immense personal satisfaction from the realization of his art in performance. "What a thing it is to have power," he confided to Catherine after reducing his friend, the eminent tragedian Macready, to tears during the private reading of *The Chimes*. Many who went to his readings were already familiar with his books, but the readings enabled him to reach a wider audience, including those who could not read at all. He always insisted that the price of some tickets for his readings should be accessible to working class patrons—and thus inadvertently facilitated the activities of scalpers, who resold tickets at inflated prices.

From the outset of his career, Dickens enjoyed reading aloud from his writing to family and friends; as we have seen, he raced back to London from Italy in 1844 to give two private readings of *The Chimes*. In 1853, he gave his first public reading, for charity, in Birmingham, where he read *A Christmas Carol* in its entirety—a performance which took over three hours—and it was always a Christmas book he chose for charity readings. When he commenced reading for profit, however, he expanded his repertoire, selecting shorter pieces such as "The Poor Traveller" and "Boots at the Holly Tree Inn," and devising routines from selected passages featuring Mrs. Gamp and Little Paul Dombey. Soon he added "The Trial from Pickwick" and a selection from *Nickleby*. Although he continued to edit *All the Year Round* during these years, he avoided substantial reading commitments while writing novels, taking time out from reading while he was composing *Great Expectations* in 1860 and *Our Mutual Friend* from 1863 through to 1865. His programs generally consisted of two pieces read over two hours.

All of the readings were taken from his early novels or from later works written in the vein of the early work. The emphasis was on comedy and pathos, omitting social criticism, and one of his most popular readings, derived from *Copperfield*, featured the storm and the drowning of Ham and Steerforth. Eventually, for his farewell tour of 1869-70, and against the advice of friends and doctors, he devised the most famous of his readings, the murder of Nancy from *Oliver Twist*, which electrified audiences but required such emotional energy to deliver that it took a fatal toll on his health.

In London, Dickens initially performed in St Martin's Hall and later in Hanover Square Rooms, eventually settling on St James's Hall. He undertook tours through the provinces, Ireland and Scotland, but although he had always found traveling by train exhilarating, in 1865, while returning from France with Ellen and her mother, he was involved in a serious accident. Work on the line left a section of track uplifted, the foreman having misread the schedule and the train on which Dickens was traveling hurtled into a ravine. Several people were killed, and he helped comfort the injured and dying, before clambering back into the carriage he had been riding in—which was teetering precariously—to retrieve the manuscript of his work in progress on *Our Mutual Friend.* Badly shaken, he became fearful of trains afterwards. He rejected the idea of undertaking a reading tour of Australia, but in 1867–68 he paid a second visit to North America. He had mellowed considerably from the fiery altercations there a quarter of a century earlier, and renewed old friendships, but his health deteriorated seriously. He never fully recovered, and on doctors' orders had to cut short his farewell tour two years later. He died of a massive stroke in June 1870, three months after his final performance. He was only 58 years old but looked like an old man.

11. Last works

*A*ll the *Year Round* featured serial fiction as its leading feature, and the first novel to appear in its pages was A *Tale of Two Cities*. Dickens's subject, the French Revolution (1789–1799), cast a long shadow throughout Europe far into the 19th century. Subsequent revolutions in France in 1830 and 1848 demonstrated, in Dickens's opinion, that the French were "always at it." England had avoided a bloody revolution of its own, but opposition to the Poor Law, Chartist riots, anti-corn law agitation, and Sunday trading riots in Hyde Park were cause for foreboding. Writing to Austen Layard in 1855, Dickens judged that conditions in England were "like the general mind of France before the breaking out of the first Revolution . . . so much the worse for smouldering instead of blazing openly," and, therefore, likely to ignite "such a Devil of a conflagration as has never been beheld since."

His principal source for the novel was Carlyle's "wonderful book" *The French Revolution* (1837), which Dickens claimed in 1851 to be reading "for the 500th time." More important than its detail is the apocalyptic vision of history, which Dickens shared with Carlyle and had previously dramatized in *Barnaby Rudge*.

Dickens drew on Ellen Ternan for his depiction of Lucie Manette; Lucie's father's disability reflects Dickens's long-standing conviction that solitary confinement was a "dreadful punishment . . . immeasurably worse than any torture of the body." The pairing of Carton and Darnay—their initials combining, tellingly, as "CD"—explores a fascination with doubles also found in Shakespeare's *Twelfth Night*, James Hogg's *Confessions and Private Memoirs of a Justified Sinner*, Alexandre Dumas' *Corsican Brothers*, and later in Robert Louis Stevenson's *Jekyll and Hyde*. Carton himself evokes a new level of sympathetic engagement by Dickens with a deeply flawed character, a fascination seen again in Eugene Wrayburn, in *Our Mutual Friend*.

In A *Tale of Two Cities*, Dickens experimented with a different approach to story-telling, which he called "picturesque," showing "characters true to nature, but whom the story itself should express, more than they should express themselves in dialogue." Readers' opinions have been divided over whether this method—eschewing Dickens's skillful evocation of a wide range of speech patterns in his other fiction—is entirely successful; many have lamented the absence of his trademark grotesquely comic characters, but the ever-accelerating velocity of the plot and lurid depiction of the Terror have made it one of his most widely read titles.

In the *Lazy Tour*, Francis Goodchild, the character drawn by Dickens from his own life, responds to the song "Annie Laurie" by scoffing at the notion of dying for love: "Lay him doon and dee! Finely he'd show off before the girl by doing *that*. A Sniveller! Why couldn't he get up, and punch somebody's head?" That remark can serve to clarify Carton's final action in the *Tale*. Although he is dissipated and world-weary throughout, the substitution of himself for Darnay as a victim of the guillotine is the very reverse of nihilism. Instead, rescuing the husband of the woman he loves is an ultimate act of bravery, and it is a "far better thing"—not simply as a personal sacrifice, but also as a prophetic vision of a better future for mankind, as upbeat an ending as any Dickens ever wrote.

When Dickens completed A *Tale of Two Cities* in 1859, he embarked on a new series of sketches under the title *The Uncommercial Traveller*. While his previous sketch-writing at the outset of his career had largely effaced the persona of Boz, the new series boldly foregrounded the character of the speaker and moved from plural to singular narration—from "we" to "I." Several of the new sketches are closely autobiographical and have often been read—mistakenly—as straightforwardly literal reports of his own childhood. As ever in his writing, Dickens drew on his own experiences but filtered them through his imagination. The title introduces the narrator, a traveler who is not commercial—that is, he is not a traveling salesman—but a flâneur—someone who moves about idly, reporting what he sees. The posed tone of these sketches–thoughtful, alert, and humane–places them among Dickens's most distinguished journalistic writings.

They are also important in his artistic evolution as experiments in narration, combining the emotions and perceptions of a child's experience with the wise retrospection of the same events by the same character as an adult. It is a method Dickens triumphantly developed in his next novel, *Great Expectations*, in which he vividly evoked the immediacy of Pip's experiences as a boy simultaneously with his later reflective retrospection, often radically at odds with what he thought and felt in the first place. Of all Dickens's novels, this one is richest in the telling.

Like *Hard Times* nearly a decade previously, the timing and format of *Great Expectations* were determined not on artistic grounds but for economic reasons. Sales of *All the Year Round* were dropping ominously when readers did not like the current serialized novel appearing in its pages, *A Day's Ride* by Charles Lever. In order to rescue his periodical, Dickens promptly jettisoned his plans to write a novel published at a later date in his preferred format of 20 monthly parts, choosing instead to transform the work immediately into shorter length in weekly installments, *Great Expectations* took over as the lead serial, leaving *A Day's Ride* to limp along to its conclusion in second place. As with previous works in this format, he found the weekly deadlines difficult, but the writing went more smoothly than for any other of his novels, producing a fast-moving narrative and an admirable overarching structure.

Great Expectations represents the most fashionable mode for fiction of the time, the sensation novel. This form, epitomized by Wilkie Collins's *Woman in White*, Mary Elizabeth Braddon's *Lady Audley's Secret*, and Ellen Wood's *East Lynne*, presented seemingly commonplace characters caught up in thrilling plots centered on crime, mystery, and mistaken identity. The combination of ordinary and extraordinary generated considerable frisson, to which Dickens added social and psychological insight and allegorical representation of moral issues, making this novel the supreme example of the form.

Great Expectations is one of only two of Dickens's novels narrated entirely in the first person, and to make certain he did not repeat himself, he re-read the other one, *David Copperfield*, "and was affected by it to a degree you would hardly believe." The story is set in the scenes of his boyhood in rural Kent, to which he had recently returned when he moved out of London to take up occupancy at Gad's Hill Place. But while some of David Copperfield's experiences closely mirror Dickens's own, Pip's life is close to Dickens's not in detail but, rather, as a spiritual autobiography, portraying a sensitive boy's aspirations for wealth and love. The later book is also, in the words of one critic, "a representative fable of the age," depicting the emergence of Victorian civilization out of Regency roughness. Pip's aspirations to better himself are not (as is sometimes claimed) snobbery so much as an effort to improve his lot through education, social refinement, and material advancement. In trying to progress, Pip turns his back on Joe, the one wholly good person from his past, and he discovers to his dismay that both love and wealth derive ultimately from exploitation: not from the genteel Miss Havisham but from Magwitch, the despised criminal who has made his fortune in the colonies. And when Pip attempts to abandon what he had so fervently sought, he retreats only to discover that Biddy, the girl back home who always loved him, has married Joe. A return to the past, the story shows, is closed off irrevocably.

Great Expectations is a curiously self-reflexive novel, in that Dickens seems to renounce the very style which had been the hallmark of his success. Viewing Miss Havisham first as a witch and then a fairy godmother, and Magwitch as an ogre who turns out to have a heart of gold, Pip must learn through hard experience to recognize that they are not larger than life fantasy figures, Dickensian grotesques as conceived in his imagination, but that each is an embittered and fallible, yet ultimately well-meaning human being. It is an apt testimony to Dickens's ultimate achievement as a writer that this late novel calls into question the very qualities which make this work so compelling; in fact, it calls into question the methods of characterization, which were distinctive in his earlier work. In addition to the probing artistry of his greatest work, it has all the comic exuberance of his early writing—the opening scenes between Pip and Joe, Dickens judged, were "droll;" the boastfulness of Pumblechook, the taunting of Pip by Trabb's boy, the theatrical tribulations of Wopsle, and the wedding of Wemmick with Miss Skiffins, are among the most exquisite comic scenes he ever wrote. *Bleak House* may be Dickens's supreme achievement, but *Great Expectations* has—in addition to great depth—a delicacy of its own.

In contrast to the speed and ease with which he wrote *Great Expectations*, his last completed novel was slow in gestation and labored in composition. *Our Mutual Friend* marks Dickens's final return to the 20-part monthly serial, which had been the mode of *Pickwick* and the majority of works that followed. Like them, it boasts a large, diverse cast, a variety of social and psychological themes, multiple plots, and with the river and the dust heaps, not one but two central unifying symbols, both complex and far-reaching. From the outset, the river is shown to be a source of livelihood—and life—as well as of death; the dust-heaps are great, obscene piles of waste and the source of great wealth.

Like *Great Expectations*, *Our Mutual Friend* taps into motifs of sensation fiction, with murder, violence, and mistaken identity disrupting the lives of seemingly ordinary people. Neither Harmon nor Boffin in disguise conveys the extraordinary sense of reversal of Magwitch's return—at once thoroughly prepared for and utterly surprising in the earlier novel. One-legged Silas Wegg is perhaps the nastiest comic grotesque figure Dickens ever conceived, and the bone articulator Mr. Venus, "floating his powerful mind in tea," is certainly the most bizarre. The good Jew Riah was introduced to redress the "great wrong" Dickens was accused of committing decades previously in emphasizing the Jewishness of Fagin, and Betty Higden's terror of the Poor Law reprises another issue from *Oliver Twist*. The satire on the vacuity of the Veneerings, the Podsnaps, and the rest of society, is the most scathing of all Dickens's works, and the innocent elopement of Bella with her father, inspired no doubt by Dickens's own love for his daughter Katey, is utterly charming.

The love themes are complex and varied. Bella is taught the folly of valuing wealth above character, while Lizzie, running away rather than succumbing to the blandishments of the careless man she secretly loves, proves to be the one woman on Earth capable of saving that lover's life, thanks to her background as an oarswoman for her scavenger father. Twemlow's praise of her after she has married Eugene is the most defiant instance of class criticism Dickens ever wrote.

But the most compelling element in the novel is the love Bradley Headstone and Eugene Wrayburn have for the same woman, a rivalry, which seems to stand on its head some of Dickens's most deeply-felt convictions. Bradley, a hard-working schoolteacher, attempting to better himself through education, seems precisely the sort of figure whom Dickens would champion; Eugene, on the other hand, is a lazy idler who moves in social circles far above anything Bradley can aspire to, indulging his attraction to Lizzie without serious concern for her virtue. He seems by contrast to represent attitudes that Dickens held in deepest scorn. And yet, the intensity of Bradley's passion is shown to be selfish and murderous, whereas Eugene undergoes a symbolic rebirth when he is very nearly killed by Bradley, and survives to make an honest woman of Lizzie after all.

Our Mutual Friend inspired the Norwegian writer and Dickens's contemporary Henrik Ibsen to pick up, in The Doll's House, on Bella's cry that she does not want her life to be that of a doll in a doll's house. Later, T. S. Eliot's collage of voices in The Waste Land explicitly referred in draft to Sloppy's ability to read aloud "in different voices;" more pervasively in the structure of the same poem, Eliot worked variations on Dickens's use of the Thames as a central structural and thematic symbol.

12. Coda: The Inimitable Boz

In 1869, Dickens began work on his last, unfinished novel. Perhaps on account of his poor health, or simply in recognition of changing patterns of publication, his contract specified a novel of only 12 monthly parts, instead of the usual 20. He wrote slowly, fearing that he was using up material faster than planned. But the completed portion of *The Mystery of Edwin Drood,*–exactly half of the projected whole–has intrigued readers ever since. Despite posthumous hints from Dickens's entourage, who claimed he had given them the outline of the full plot, no one knows for sure how the story would have ended, or even whether Edwin actually was indeed murdered.

Dickens's eldest son, Charley, affirmed that this father had assured him that Edwin was dead. Forster reported that the story was conceived as the murder of a nephew by an uncle, and that "the originality was to consist in the review of the murderer's career by himself at the close, when its temptations were to be dwelt upon as if, not he the culprit, but some other man, were the tempted." Luke Fildes, the book's illustrator, claimed that Dickens put great importance on Jasper's scarf, which was to be revealed as the murder weapon, and that the story would end with Jasper in a condemned cell. Of the many conclusions proposed by readers and completions of the story by other hands, some accept these statements and others do not.

The opening scene in an opium den draws on Dickens's police-escorted nocturnal tours, and he was certainly aware of Thomas de Quincey's *Confessions of an English Opium Eater*, as well as of Wilkie Collins's *The Moonstone*. He had been fascinated for many years by animal magnetism, as mesmerism was then called, and he counted Dr. John Elliotson, who gave public demonstrations of the phenomenon in the 1830s, among his friends. While in Italy in the

1840s, he attempted to cure Mme Augusta de la Rue of a nervous disorder by means of mesmerism.

Cloisterham is clearly modeled on Rochester, near his childhood home, and is the setting for Mr. Pickwick's first adventures when he leaves London. Neville and Helena Landless, arriving from Ceylon, introduce issues of race and empire, and the identity of Dick Datchery, who is clearly in disguise, is a matter of endless dispute.

On the day before he died, Dickens wrote the following passage:

> A brilliant morning shines on the old city. Its antiquities and ruins are surpassingly beautiful, with the lusty ivy gleaming in the sun, and the rich trees waving in the balmy air. Changes of glorious light from the moving boughs, songs of birds, scents from gardens, woods, and fields—or, rather, from the one great garden of the whole cultivated island in its yielding time—penetrate into the Cathedral, subdue its earthy odour, and preach the Resurrection and the Life. The cold stone tombs of centuries ago grow warm; and flecks of brightness dart into the sternest marble corners of the building, fluttering there like wings.

These words seem the fitting finale to an energetic life, dwelling, as they do, on last thoughts and images while the author was unknowingly on the brink of death. But perhaps even more indicative of the man Dickens really was are the very last words he ever wrote, which follow a few lines later. Mr. Datchery, we are told, "falls to with an appetite." If ever there was a man who lived his life with "an appetite," it was Charles Dickens.

Note on Sources

Quotations from Dickens's letters are taken with permission from the Pilgrim/British Academy edition, *The Letters of Charles Dickens*, edited by Graham Storey, et al. Oxford: Clarendon Press, 1965–2002.

Quotations from John Forster, *The Life of Charles Dickens* [1872–74], are taken from the edition edited by J. W. T. Ley. London: Cecil Palmer, 1928.

Quotations from Dickens's journalism are taken from the original pages of *Household Words*, available on the website *Dickens Journals Online* and in *The Dent Uniform Edition of Dickens' Journalism*, edited by Michael Slater and John Drew. 4 volumes. London: Dent, 1995–2000.

Dickens's speeches are available in the Clarendon edition, *The Speeches of Charles Dickens*, edited by K. J. Fielding. Oxford: Clarendon, 1960, 1988. Unfortunately, they are not available for quotation.

Suggested Reading

Dickens's novels have been endlessly reprinted, and inexpensive second-hand copies and modern paperbacks are easy to find. Any unabridged copy will do, although only a modern edition is likely to print both the original and the revised ending of *Great Expectations*. In addition to the novels, readers should not overlook his *Christmas Books*, *Sketches by Boz*, and *The Uncommercial Traveller*.

See also *The Oxford Companion to Charles Dickens*, edited by Paul Schlicke. Oxford: Oxford University Press, 1999, 2000, originally published as *The Oxford Reader's Companion to Dickens*, and reissued as the Anniversary Edition, with a foreword by Simon Callow, 2011.

OTHER STUDIES

Peter Ackroyd. *Dickens*. London: Sinclair-Stevenson, 1990.

Malcolm Andrews. *Dickens and the Grown-up Child*. Basingstoke: Macmillan, 1994

_____. *Charles Dickens and His Performing Selves*. Oxford: Oxford University Press, 2006.

_____. *Dickensian Laughter*. Oxford: Oxford University Press, 2013.

John Bowen and Robert Patten, eds. *Palgrave Advances in Charles Dickens Studies*. Basingstoke: Palgrave Macmillan, 2006.

John Butt and Kathleen Tillotson. *Dickens at Work*. London: Methuen, 1957.

Simon Callow. *Charles Dickens and the Great Theatre of the World*. London: Harper, 2012.

G. K. Chesterton. *Charles Dickens*. London: Dent, 1906.

Kathryn Chittick. *Dickens and the 1830s*. Cambridge: Cambridge University Press, 1990.

Philip Collins. *Dickens and Crime*. London: Macmillan, 1962.

_____. *Dickens and Education*. London: Macmillan, 1963.

John Drew. *Dickens the Journalist*. London: Methuen, 2003.

A. E. Dyson. *The Inimitable Dickens*. London: Macmillan, 1970.

George Ford and Lauriat Lane, Jr., eds. *The Dickens Critics*. Ithaca: Cornell University Press, 1961.

Juliet John. *Dickens's Villains*. Oxford: Oxford University Press, 2001.

_____. *Dickens and Mass Culture*. Oxford: Oxford University Press, 2010.

Edgar Johnson. *Dickens: His Tragedy and Triumph*. Boston: Little, Brown, 1952.

Sally Ledger and Holly Furneaux, eds. *Charles Dickens in Context*. Cambridge: Cambridge University Press, 2011.

Lillian Nayder. *The Other Dickens: A Life of Catherine Hogarth*. Ithaca: Cornell University Press, 2010.

Robert L. Patten. *Charles Dickens and His Publishers*. Oxford: Oxford University Press, 1978

Valerie Purton. *Dickens and the Sentimental Tradition*. London: Anthem, 2012.

Ruth Richardson. *Dickens and the Workhouse*. Oxford: Oxford University Press, 2012.

Paul Schlicke. *Dickens and Popular Entertainment*. London: Allen and Unwin, 1985.

Michael Slater. *Dickens and Women*. London: Dent, 1983.

_____. *Charles Dickens: A Life Defined by Writing*. New Haven and London: Yale University Press, 2009.

Claire Tomalin. *The Invisible Woman: The Story of Nelly Ternan and Charles Dickens*. London: Viking, 1990.

About the Author

Paul Schlicke is the author of *Dickens and Popular Entertainment* and the editor of the *Oxford Companion to Charles Dickens*, and has served as president of the Dickens Society and the Dickens Fellowship, and as chairman of the trustees of the Charles Dickens Museum. Prior to his retirement in 2010, he taught English at the University of Aberdeen for 40 years.

Afterword

Thank you for reading *Simply Dickens*!

If you enjoyed reading it, we would be grateful if you could help others discover and enjoy it too.

Please review it with your favorite book provider such as Amazon, BN, Kobo, iBooks, and Goodreads, among others.

Again, thank you for your support and we look forward to offering you more great reads.

Made in the USA
Monee, IL
13 September 2020

TIME
FOR KIDS

CONFIDENT 3 READER *Science Scoops*

Butterflies!

By the Editors of TIME FOR KIDS
WITH DAVID BJERKLIE

HarperCollins*Publishers*

About the Author: David Bjerklie is a science reporter for TIME magazine. He has written articles for TIME and TIME FOR KIDS® on health, nature, and geography. The author collected fossils, bugs, and fish as a kid and studied biology and anthropology in college.

To my very favorite two butterflies in the world, Erika and Sarah.

Special thanks to science teachers everywhere.   *–D.B.*

Library of Congress Cataloging-in-Publication Data is available.

ISBN-10: 0-06-078213-7 (pbk.) — ISBN-10: 0-06-078217-X (trade)
ISBN-13: 978-0-06-078213-9 (pbk.) — ISBN-13: 978-0-06-078217-7 (trade)

16 17 18 19 20 SCP 20 19 18 17 16 15 14 13
First Edition

Photography and Illustration Credits:
Cover: Alamy; cover front flap: Chris Martin Bahr—SPL; title page: Gail M. Shumway—Bruce Coleman; contents page: Michael & Patricia Fogden—Minden; pp. 4–5: Dr. John Brackenbury—SPL; pp. 6–7: Brand X Pictures/Alamy; pg. 7 (inset): E. R. Degginger—Animals Animals; pp. 8–9: Anne Reas; pg. 9 (inset): Anne Reas; pp. 10–11: Michael & Patricia Fogden—Minden; pp. 12–13: Klaus Nigge—Foto Natura/Minden; pg. 13 (inset): Patti Murray—Animals Animals; pg. 14: Scott Camazine; pg. 15: Scott Camazine; pp. 16–17: Frans Lanting—Minden; pg. 17 (inset): Scott Camazine; pg. 17 (How Big?): Anne Reas; pp. 18–19: Robert M. Vera—Alamy; pp. 20–21: Fritz Polking—Peter Arnold; pg. 21 (How Far?): John Berg; pp. 22–23: Rod Planck—NHPA; pg. 23 (inset): Breck P. Kent—Animals Animals; pp. 24–25: James L. Amos—Corbis; pg. 25 (butterfly inset): AP; pg. 25 (Chip Taylor inset): courtesy Chip Taylor/Monarch Watch; pp. 26–27: Brian Farrell/Museum of Comparative Zoology & Harvard University; pp. 28–29: Alan Blank—Bruce Coleman/Alamy; pg. 29 (inset): Monserrate J. Schwartz—Alamy; pp. 30–31: A. H. Rider—Photo Researchers; pg. 31 (inset): Gail M. Shumway—Bruce Coleman; pg. 32 (chrysalis): Frans Lanting—Minden; pg. 32 (endangered): A. H. Rider—Photo Researchers; pg. 32 (metamorphosis): Frans Lanting—Minden; pg. 32 (migration): Fritz Polking—Peter Arnold; pg. 32 (scales): E. R. Degginger—Animals Animals; pg. 32 (spinnerets): Scott Camazine; pg. 32 (Costa Rica): Corbis; pg. 32 (Ethiopia): Nathan Brockman—Reiman Gardens; pg. 32 (France): Naturfoto Honal/Corbis; pg. 32 (Indonesia): Michael & Patricia Fogden—Minden; pg. 32 (Russia): Pat O'Hara—Corbis

Acknowledgments:
For TIME FOR KIDS: Editorial Director: Keith Garton; Editor: Nelida Gonzalez Cutler; Art Director: Rachel Smith; Photography Editor: Jill Tatara

HarperCollins books may be purchased for educational, business, or sales promotional use. For information, please e-mail: Special Markets Department at SPsales@harpercollins. com.

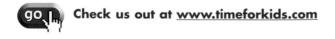

Check us out at www.timeforkids.com

CONTENTS

This tree nymph butterfly is from Indonesia.

CHAPTER ONE

Flying Flowers

Swallowtail butterflies soar over a field of flowers.

Flutter! Flutter!

Something colorful glistens in the meadow. Is it a flower? No, it's a butterfly! Its beautiful wings flutter in the air. This creature is one of the insect world's biggest showoffs!

The blue morpho lives in the rainforests of Central and South America.

The wings of the blue morpho butterfly are not really blue. But when tiny ridges on the scales reflect light, the wings appear blue.

Butterflies and moths belong to the same group of insects.

Short hairs called scales cover their wings like powder. Some scales can even make the wings appear to shimmer. Butterflies are usually more brightly colored than moths.

Take a close look at a butterfly.

Butterflies are active during the day. They hold their wings straight up while resting. There are nearly 20,000 different types of butterflies.

FOREWINGS: Butterflies have two front wings.

HIND WINGS: Butterflies have two back wings.

BODY: Butterflies' bodies are divided into three parts: the head, thorax, and abdomen.

ABDOMEN

MOTHS ARE ACTIVE AT NIGHT. They rest with their wings down and spread apart. There may be as many as 200,000 types of moths.

ANTENNAS: These thread-like sense organs have knobs at the end. Antennas are used for both touch and smell.

HEAD

EYE: Two compound eyes let butterflies see in almost every direction.

PROBOSCIS: Butterflies use their long coiled tongues to sip water or nectar from flowers.

FEET: Special organs on butterflies' feet help the insects taste what they land on!

THORAX

CHAPTER TWO

Amazing

The pierid
butterfly's eggs
look like tiny jewels.

Changes

The life of a butterfly begins in an egg. Butterflies lay eggs one at a time or in clusters. They lay their eggs only on plants that caterpillars like to eat. That's because when an egg hatches, a caterpillar comes out!

An oriole gobbles
a caterpillar.

WATCH OUT!

An eastern black
swallowtail caterpillar

A caterpillar is tiny when it hatches.

Then it begins to eat and eat. It can eat many times its own body weight every day. Caterpillars shed their skins several times. This is called molting.

But caterpillars must be careful. It is a dangerous world for them! Most end up as a meal for birds, frogs, and other insects.

A monarch
caterpillar attaches
itself to a leaf.

HANGING OUT!

The chrysalis
may hang on a
twig for weeks
or even months.

One day the caterpillar looks for
a safe spot to make a home.

Then it sheds its skin one last time. With the
help of special mouthparts, called spinnerets,
it attaches itself to a plant, twig, or leaf.
The caterpillar makes a case called a chrysalis.

The chrysalis changes color.

Inside the chrysalis an amazing change takes place.

It is called metamorphosis. First the chrysalis turns almost clear. Then it splits open. The butterfly struggles to get out. Soon it will fly!

At last the butterfly emerges.

How Big?

The Queen Alexandra birdwing, which lives in New Guinea, is the biggest butterfly. It has a wingspan of twelve inches.

The pygmy blue, which lives in the U.S., is the smallest butterfly. It has a wingspan of less than half an inch.

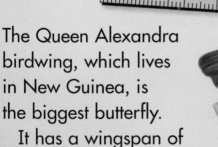

CHAPTER THREE

Migrating

Every year as many as half a billion monarchs make a long, dangerous journey south. Their migration begins at the end of summer. They need to find a new home for the winter.

Monarchs

Monarchs in California will head south.

Monarchs rest on a
fir tree in Mexico.

Many monarchs head to a mountain hideaway in Mexico.

They will spend the winter in a forest of fir trees. It is a perfect place to rest because the air is cool and moist.

For more than four months, hundreds of millions of monarchs flock in the trees. The monarchs rest and wait for winter to end.

How Far?

Canada

United States

Mexico

Monarchs are long-distance travelers. It can take one monarch up to sixty days to reach its winter home. Some travel as far as 3,000 miles!

North
West — East
South

In the spring monarchs begin the journey back north.

Some are now more than six months old. This generation of monarchs lives longer than others. Most monarchs only live for about a month!

Along the route monarchs lay eggs and die. Caterpillars hatch from these eggs. The butterflies that develop continue the trip.

A monarch caterpillar crawls on milkweed, its favorite food.

Monarch eggs

It is summertime!

Northern areas are once again filled with monarchs. These are the great-great-grandchildren of the butterflies that made the long journey to Mexico.

Soon it will be time for monarchs to head south. How do they know their way? Scientists are working to find the answer.

These monarchs are in Louisiana.

Hail to the Monarchs!

Chip Taylor thinks monarchs rule. He is a scientist who studies insects. "The monarch migration is one of the world's wonders," says Taylor. "This butterfly weighs less than a paper clip, but it can fly for two months!"

Taylor is the director of Monarch Watch. Each year thousands of volunteers tag almost 100,000 monarchs. Numbered stickers are carefully placed on butterflies' wings. Volunteers must be gentle!

If you find a tagged butterfly, report it to Monarch Watch. The information will help scientists learn more about monarchs and their long journey.

CHAPTER FOUR

Long Live

This ancient butterfly
is preserved in stone.

Butterflies!

A butterfly may look delicate, but it is one sturdy insect. Butterflies and moths fluttered in the sky when dinosaurs roamed the earth. These gentle bugs have graced our planet for more than 150 million years!

An owl butterfly
has eyespots.

Butterflies don't bite or growl.

So how do they stay safe? Some butterflies
are poisonous. Others use camouflage to
blend into their background. Butterflies
with big eyespots on their wings scare
enemies away.

Plant a Butterfly Garden!

You can help butterflies by planting a garden that attracts them. Find out what butterflies live in your region. Then grow their favorite foods. Monarchs like milkweed plants. Swallowtails love pipevine. Many butterflies enjoy marigolds, bee balm, coneflowers, lilacs, and peonies.

Butterflies are attracted to bright colors. Purple, yellow, white, blue, and red are their favorites. Butterflies also enjoy sipping fruit juice. Watermelon, mashed ripe bananas, or strawberries make good snacks.

A yellow swallowtail lands on a marigold.

One hundred years ago, there were more butterflies than today.

Many species are endangered or extinct. We need to work to keep butterflies in our world!

Did You Know?

 Butterflies live everywhere except Antarctica.

Butterflies cannot fly unless the temperature is above 60° F.

Most butterflies fly at a speed of about 5 miles per hour. But some can fly as fast as 30 miles per hour!

Some male butterflies are often so busy finding mates that they do not have time to eat.

Many adult butterflies sip nectar from flowers. They help spread pollen from flower to flower. This helps flowers make seeds.

The karner blue butterfly is endangered.

WORDS  to Know

Chrysalis:
the protective case in which metamorphosis takes place

Migration
a seasonal journey

Endangered:
animals or plants in danger of dying out, or becoming extinct

Scales:
the tiny hairs th cover a butterf wings

Metamorphosis:
the change by which a caterpillar becomes a butterfly

Spinneret
special mouthparts that help a caterpillar ma a chrysalis

FUN FACTS HOW DO YOU SAY BUTTERFLY

1

In **Costa Rica**, a butterfly is called a mariposa.

2

In **Ethiopia**, a butterfly is called a birrabirro.

3

In **France**, a butterfly is called a papillon.

4

In **Indonesia**, a butterfly is called a kupu-kupu.

5

In **Russia** butterfly called a babochk